The King's Daughter Dances

To Eleanora,
who knows the King

Frances Riley

The King's Daughter Dances

The Susan Ray Story

Frances J. Riley

PROVIDENCE HOUSE PUBLISHERS
Franklin, Tennessee

Library of Congress Catalog Card Number: 97-75447

ISBN: 1-57736-081-8

Cover design by Gary Bozeman

Book title and poem "The King's Daughter Dances" by permission of Betty D. Mojica

PROVIDENCE HOUSE PUBLISHERS
238 Seaboard Lane • Franklin, Tennessee 37067
800-321-5692

Contents

Foreword

Word came to me of this most unusual story about a very unusual Christian disciple, one who received and responded to the call of God in spite of what might appear to most of us as insurmountable difficulties.

Susan Ray is a perfect example of how God can provide the "how" if a Christian will merely say "yes" to His call. Susan was a quadriplegic from the age of four, the victim of a devastating polio epidemic. With God's help and the creativity of dedicated Christian parents, Dr. and Mrs. Cecil Ray, she wrote books, tracts, and filmstrip manuals, spoke to groups that would make most preachers' knees shake, and called and wrote letters to corporate and government leaders to challenge them to do better.

In living out her calling, she ministered to children and adults in two languages, witnessed to her younger brother as well as to other friends and strangers, and lived out in her own life a committed stewardship of God's blessings and calling. She was an evangelist and missionary extraordinaire.

The reader of this biography will be challenged to seek God's will for his or her own life and may very well laugh and cry in the process. I am happy to commend this book to you.

BILLY GRAHAM
MONTREAT, NORTH CAROLINA

Tribute

"Missionary Extraordinaire" is the most descriptive term I know to characterize Susan Ray. A Christian activist in the best sense of that word, Susan had a lust for life born of her relationship with Jesus Christ and an insatiable desire to share the Good News of the Gospel with all people everywhere.

As a young adult, she witnessed to and worked with Mexican Americans in the River Country of Texas, as well as with children and youth in her home church. After coming to North Carolina, where her father, Cecil Ray, was executive director of the Baptist State Convention, Susan began a ministry through the "Big A Club" with the children in the apartments near her church, Crabtree Valley Baptist Church. At Crabtree, she was a leader of the children and youth in missions education and missions projects.

Susan's passion for missions perhaps is captured best in the numerous books and articles that she wrote. The **Baptist Way Series**, which she authored and customized for Baptist conventions in Texas, North Carolina, and Florida, **Cooperation: The Baptist Way to a Lost World**, and other books that she wrote reveal her commitment to Christian stewardship that places missions, ministry, and proclamation of the Gospel as top priorities for her life.

It was totally incidental to Susan that she was a quadriplegic; she never used her condition as an excuse. God compensated for her physical limitations with an extra measure of mental, social, and spiritual consciousness.

For more than forty years, Susan was an example, an inspiration, and a challenge to all who knew her. What an impact she made for time and eternity. Her story will bless all who read these pages.

ROY J. SMITH
EXECUTIVE DIRECTOR-TREASURER
BAPTIST STATE CONVENTION OF NORTH CAROLINA

Introduction

Dance is perhaps the most ancient and yet the most completely preserved of the arts. It seems that people have always danced, both alone and together. They have danced for joy; they have danced in celebration. People have danced to express their gratitude to their gods, to appease their gods, and to make appeals to their gods for rain, for abundant crops, or for deliverance from their enemies. They have danced after a long-sought victory, and they have danced to express their mourning at the passing of a national or cultural hero. They have even danced in celebration of the change of seasons.

Ancient dances apparently were not for entertainment but were to help the tribe or culture survive. Long before people passed their traditions down by the written word, they were sharing their history and culture through oral tradition and, surprising as it may seem to some, through the tribal dance.

Dancing is defined as the moving of one's feet or body or both rhythmically to the accompaniment of music. "Dance" is also used to refer to a bodily action such as to leap or skip from excitement or emotion. When we hear the word "dance," our minds may envision anything from soaring ballet leaps to the simple swaying at a long-ago high school prom to the graceful waltz of a nineteenth-century ball or even the exuberant square dance. But regardless of the image that fills one's mind when he or she hears the word"dance," the common element for everyone would likely be the musically accompanied rhythmic movement of the body.

Many Christian people do not dance because they have come to believe that somehow it is sinful. Other Christians do not dance for fear they will be frowned upon by their brethren. However, dancing played an essential role in Hebrew life in biblical times. Ecclesiastes taught that "there is a time to mourn and a time to dance."

Almost a dozen expressions in the Old Testament describe dancing. Though most references to dancing occur on sacred occasions, not all of them do. Perhaps a sort of mixed sacred/secular occasion is represented by the dancing of Miriam and her handmaids in celebration of the crossing of the Red Sea. The Bible also portrays the joyous folk dancing of the workers in the vineyards of Shiloh at the vintage festival. Whatever the occasion, dancing was an expression of celebration and/or praise. David danced before the Ark of the Covenant when it was brought into Jerusalem, its true home as far as David was concerned. And, in the New Testament, the return of the prodigal son was a cause for celebration and dancing.

Many people do not dance, in the popular sense of the word, because they are shy, or say they have two left feet, or think it is sinful, or because they are physically incapable of doing so. Susan Ray would have fitted into this last group. She had a joyful heart and mind, well-suited to dancing, which she never lost. But, when she was four years old, she lost the physical ability to dance when she was stricken with polio in the worst and last polio epidemic in America. And it struck the young—those who understood it least but probably accepted it best—far more frequently than it did older people.

In that dread year of 1952, thousands of families were startled by the rapid onslaught of this dread disease as it struck one of their children. The young Ray family was among them. Lanny was an infant and was constantly entertained and fawned over by his four-year-old sister, Susan. Susan was an active, articulate playmate for Lanny, and she was filled with curiosity and adventurous thoughts.

Susan had the sort of indomitable spirit that is usually celebratory; she would have danced with joy and praise on many occasions had she been physically able to do so. This is her story, told as she lived it— humbly and triumphantly—with the hope that someone will be blessed by something she said or wrote or did.

Susan would celebrate, sing praises, and dance with joy to know that someone has been inspired or challenged to new heights by reading her story. Dance with Susan as you read.

James Clark
Nashville, Tennessee

The King's Daughter Dances

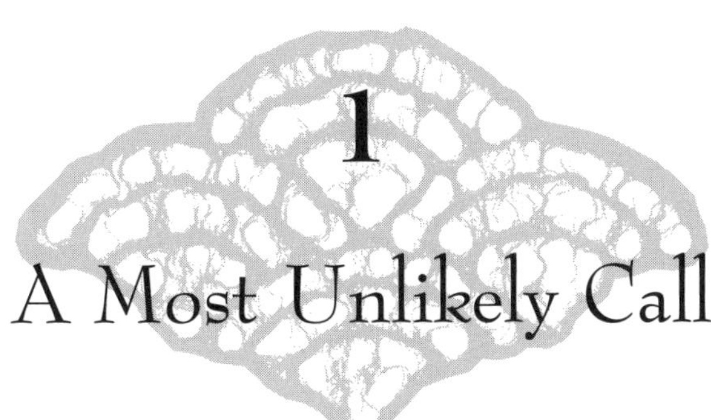

A Most Unlikely Call

Mid-summer sunlight streamed through the windows of New Mexico Hall as more than a hundred young people heard a closing speaker challenge them to full-time mission service:

If you feel God speaking to you, deep in your inmost heart, then you must answer. To do nothing is to say "No" to His call. So, with all heads bowed and eyes closed, search your hearts to know God's will for you and missions.

As the pianist played softly, they began singing a familiar hymn that most of them knew by heart:

We've a story to tell to the nations,
That shall turn their hearts to the right
A story of truth and mercy
A story of peace and light.

It was a solemn time of decision and dedication for these youths who were attending Home Missions Week at Glorieta Conference Centers. They had come to learn first hand about missions, had listened to and come to know missionaries and some of the people whose lives had been changed through missions This was the climax of that experience as they were challenged to offer their lives to missions as well.

We've a song to be sung to the nations,
That shall lift their hearts to the Lord
A song that shall conquer evil
And shatter the spear and sword.

Slowly, one or two at a time, some youth began going forward to the front of the auditorium. Many approached timidly, as if unsure of their decision; others went quickly, almost skipping, their faces radiant with purpose.

> We've a Savior to show to the nations
> Whom the path of sorrow hath trod,
> That all of the world's great peoples
> Might come to the truth of God
> For the darkness shall turn to dawning,
> And the dawning to noonday bright
> And Christ's great kingdom shall come to earth,
> A kingdom of love and light.

A soft voice spoke breathlessly from the back of the room. "I want to go down too, Becky. Will you push me please?"

"Oh, Susan! Are you sure?"

"Yes, I'm sure! Please roll me down to the front."

So, accompanied by the soft whish of rubber-tired wheels and the final notes of a hymn, eleven-year-old Susan Ray stepped out on faith to give her life to missions.

Susan's brother, Lanny, and three of her friends who were with her that day had not been prepared for this decision, but, knowing Susan, they were not too surprised. Even though she was young, she was very much a person who knew her own mind.

For each of those making decisions that day, life held many roadblocks and challenges, but not as many as would face Susan as she worked out her calling. Here was a mission volunteer who could not sit erect, walk, or even breathe on her own; Susan was a respiratory quadriplegic, almost totally paralyzed by polio!

Eleven might seem too early an age for one to make such a momentous decision, but Susan was quite mature in her thinking. As the daughter of a Texas Baptist pastor and his mission-minded wife, she had been acquainted with the needs of Christian missions all of her life. Program personnel at that Glorieta experience may have felt that she would not be able to carry out her calling, but they did not know Susan. God knew her heart and gave her a unique ministry which allowed her to serve Him throughout a lifetime, which, in spite of difficulties, was full and rich. The things Susan accomplished and the variety of ministries she supported and served made her a most extraordinary missionary, indeed.

The story of any commitment cannot be separated from the climate in which that commitment evolved. Thus, Susan's story cannot be told except in the context of her family and the conditions that existed at that time in our nation's history.

Susan and family just four months before polio struck.

Susan Ray had not always been a victim of polio. Until stricken, she was a normal four year old who scampered all over the house, rode her trike, and crawled alongside her baby brother, Lanny. In reality, she was but one of thousands whose lives were deeply affected by polio.

Classified as a respiratory polio quadriplegic, having only a slight bit of movement in her right hand and arm, and also in her right leg and foot, Susan was one of the more than sixty thousand cases which occurred during the 1952 epidemic. There were over three thousand deaths, and hundreds of Americans were left badly diminished in opportunity for a normal life. Texas was hit hardest of all.

Life for Cecil and Charlene Ray and their two children changed radically the morning of February 27, 1952.

CHARLENE. I was awakened in the early morning by Susan crying and kicking her legs violently in her bed next to ours. Her pediatrician had treated her a few days before for what he believed was an ear infection. "Are your ears hurting again?" I asked as I hurried to her.

"No, my back!" she cried. "My back hurts!"

By this time, Cecil was up and getting our baby, Lanny, out of his crib. I took Lanny, Cecil lifted Susan carefully, and we all went to the kitchen where I hurriedly prepared breakfast before reaching the doctor. Susan ate nothing.

"Bring her in as soon as I'm open," the doctor directed. So we prepared for the trip.

I noticed how limp Susan was as I dressed her. She hardly moved as I struggled to get her clothes on. At last we were ready! Cecil took Susan to the car and laid her carefully on the back seat. We rushed to the doctor, fretting at the slow rush-hour traffic.

As the doctor examined her, he shook his head and frowned. He went back again to her arms and legs, lifting and fingering along their entire length. Then he turned to us and said solemnly, "We must get Susan to the hospital immediately."

My heart sank as I realized the seriousness of his expression. "Oh, no!" I thought. "Susan has the flu or maybe even pneumonia."

If only it had been one of those!

CECIL. Susan had been sick for about five days and, on first seeing the doctor, had been diagnosed with an ear infection. When she awoke that morning with a backache, neither Charlene nor I even suspected such a thing as polio. It was winter and polio was a disease of summer. But when he saw Susan that February morning, Dr. Jenkins recognized that it was polio, indeed.

CHARLENE. The next couple of hours were a nightmare. We rushed Susan to the hospital where they began to work over her feverishly. There was the spinal tap which, I learned later, had to be taken to learn if a person had polio. I remember the nurse hurrying in to whisper something to the doctor who nodded toward the door and gestured to her to hurry. My heart sank even further. I noted how often he was checking Susan's chest and respiration, timing her breaths, and listening again and again. As everyone rushed around frantically, our apprehension grew. This looked to be very serious!

Then suddenly the Lubbock firemen came rushing into the room with an iron lung. Susan's diaphragm was becoming paralyzed—she had respiratory polio!

By the time the firemen had arrived, Susan had become pale as a ghost and her lips had a bluish tinge. Even I could see that she needed air badly and could not breathe it into her small body without help. When

Lanny and Susan, both busy and active before polio struck Susan.

they rushed the big Emerson tank respirator into the room, a flurry of activity began.

Open the tank—put sheets on the bed inside—pull the neck collar gasket open—lay Susan inside and push her head through the collar—stuff cotton around her neck to ensure an airtight seal—release the collar and make sure it all fit snugly—close the tank—click the switch—set the gauges—and hold your own breath while waiting to see if everything worked. I thought they would never get it all done!

The firemen did most of the work with help from the nurses. The doctor set the gauges, one for rate of respiration and one for the amount of pressure needed to pull sufficient air into Susan's lungs. Slowly, a bit of color began to creep into her face and lips. She roused and looked around, obviously glad to be breathing again.

CECIL. When we learned at the doctor's that Susan would be admitted to the hospital, I had gone back home to pick up some things she would need. When I returned and saw that giant metal lung engulfing Susan's frail body, I was stunned beyond speech. I struggled to comprehend and accept the fact that Susan was gravely ill, perhaps to the point of death. How could a happy, very active child become so limp and so ill in such a few hours? Gradually, the impact of what I saw and felt came over me, and the rest of that day was a daze as I struggled to comprehend how swiftly our lives had been changed forever.

After a couple of hours, when I saw that Susan was able to breathe adequately, I went back home to start calling our family and friends to rally prayer support. I knew we needed God's strength and wisdom to a degree we had never known before.

Charlene's parents had been called as soon as we arrived at the hospital and had gotten Lanny and taken him home, so we knew he was receiving good care. When I called my parents, my mother answered the phone but made no comment at all as I told her.

"Do you understand what I'm saying, Mother?" I asked. "They tell us that Susan has polio."

After a long silence she replied, "Yes, I understand. I just don't know how to respond." You see, mother and daddy had already faced the sorrow of having four children die. They knew all too well the pain of a child seriously ill.

"What can we do, Son. Should we come there? What would be the most help to you and Charlene right now?"

"Your prayers are our greatest need right now, Mother," I replied. I knew my parents were devout Christians and believed, as we did, that even in the darkest hours, God was there.

2

The Polio Plague

Early reports of poliomyelitis describe a disease which usually began with a fever, some achiness and malaise, and often ended with paralysis, especially in children. Perhaps the earliest hint of the disease is depicted on an ancient Egyptian tile showing a man with a withered leg walking with a cane. There was an epidemic of polio in Sweden in 1905, but almost nothing was known about how it was spread and how to treat it. In Vienna, two research scientists, Earl Popper and Karl Landsteiner, first demonstrated that polio is a viral disease which can be passed from humans to monkeys, but real progress in understanding the nature of polio was slow. Epidemics continued to pop up sporadically with no discernible pattern, although records as early as 1789 refer to small outbreaks. On an average, polio claimed the lives of six out of every one hundred cases. Polio first surfaced in America in New York in 1916, with twenty-seven thousand diagnosed cases and six thousand deaths. No hospital wanted to admit polio victims, so a new hospital, dedicated to dealing solely with contagious diseases, was begun and completed in a little over a week. It was constructed by volunteers under the direction of professional builders and the Carpenters' Union.

Fear of the disease spreading so dominated the minds of everyone that by 1939 there were only three hundred hospitals in the entire nation that would accept polio patients. American physicians such as Dr. Simon Flexner, who directed the Rockefeller Institute for Medical Research, were publishing the results of their research, but progress was slow. In 1946, there were twenty-five thousand cases in America. In 1953, thirty-five thousand people were stricken. By 1957, when the Salk vaccine was being used, there were only five thousand cases. By 1960, the year before the Sabin oral polio vaccine was introduced, the number of cases nation-wide had dropped to three thousand.

The worst polio epidemic in American history occurred in 1952, and Texas had the most cases of any state in the nation; however, 1952 was only one of the forty years during which epidemics kept Americans in virtual imprisonment each summer from June through September. No one knew what caused polio, but suppositions abounded. Pools, parks, and theaters were closed. Attendance at churches and synagogues fell as families isolated themselves, afraid that exposure to others would cause the disease to spread. Nothing seemed to make a difference.

Diseases such as typhoid and cholera had been successfully routed with strong soaps, boiling water, and heightened sanitation. The concept of public health had spread the gospel of fresh air, clean food, and pure water. None of these were effective where polio was concerned. It struck without discrimination and preyed most frequently on children.

Mothers were urged to sterilize the tops of milk bottles before opening, put chlorine bleach in bath water, and be sure no flies came into the house. At that time, it was strongly believed that removing children's tonsils would prevent ear and throat infections and protect against the repeated strep infections some children experienced. No doctor, however, would dare perform surgery of any kind during those dread summer months because it was also believed that removing the tonsils left a child more vulnerable to polio and that surgery would weaken a child, setting him up for infections. So the medical profession was hard put to know what procedure to follow. Postponing all such operations until late fall, however, made no real difference. Nothing stemmed the sporadic outbreaks that made American summers a nightmare.

Susan Ray was only four and a half when she contracted polio. As an adult, she could not remember her early years when she romped with friends and played with her baby brother. Not remembering may have been a blessing for her, but her parents remembered and it hurt!

CHARLENE. By the second or third day after Susan was admitted to the hospital in Lubbock, we recognized that nursing help would be some-what scarce. Little was known about how polio was spread, and most of the nurses were fearful they would take it home to their own families. We called Cecil's sister, Mary Ruth Cervenka, in Rowena, Texas, who came for two weeks to help us, leaving her husband and two children to pretty much fend for themselves. Mary Ruth read to Susan, sang songs with her, and played simple games. With additional help from our friend, Stella Herod, we managed pretty well during the day, and Cecil, together with a special nurse, stayed at night. Having that special nurse helped Cecil get some sleep and allowed me time at home with Lanny.

CECIL. It is difficult to describe our feelings during those first weeks. For the first twenty-four hours, we were literally in shock. Still, in the midst of all that was wrong, we were deeply blessed. We had the best of friends, a concerned and caring medical team, the abilities of those firemen who knew how to tend and repair Susan's iron lung, a very supportive family, and a loving church family as well. Yet, with all this and our faith in a loving, omnipotent God, we still felt inadequate to meet Susan's needs and to be able to provide her with continuing care. The growing realization that no one around us had had much experience with treating respiratory polio made us fearful. It was not until later, when we took Susan to the special respiratory center in Houston, that we realized there were only a few hospitals in the nation whose medical staffs specialized in the type of care she needed.

Shortly before Susan was stricken, we had bought her a new record, "Here Comes Peter Cottontail." This was her all-time favorite. She had us bring it and her record player to the hospital, where she had it played for her, over and over again. For years afterward, when I would hear that little song, a deep feeling of sadness would come over me. Instead of hearing a happy little tune, I remembered those sad and hopeless days when we did not even know if our little girl would live.

The Rays' uneasiness at the overall lack of experience in the use of the iron lung was justified. During the early decades of polio outbreaks in America, firemen were the primary group trained in the use and upkeep of these metal monsters. There was usually an iron lung stored among the equipment at fire stations in large communities. Not that the firemen knew much about the specifics of respiratory paralysis or the ratio of breaths to age and size. They simply knew something about the mechanics of how the lungs worked. However, as outbreaks of polio continued, fire and rescue units, as well as the medical community, developed more and better ways of assisting those who were stricken.

CECIL. Our sudden dependence on an iron lung, something we had usually seen in pictures and news stories, was frightening. I had frequently visited with James Herod the year before, and his was the only iron lung Charlene and I had seen in use. The son of Stella Herod, our church's nursery worker, James had contracted polio two years prior to Susan and at first was paralyzed in both his legs and his diaphragm. Later, however, he had been able to overcome his breathing problem, and only his legs remained paralyzed.

Knowing that Susan's life depended on a little-understood machine increased our uneasiness. Bit by bit, we realized that neither our doctor nor the nurses had much experience with an iron lung. In fact, some had never even seen one prior to seeing Susan's. Only the firemen knew something—mostly about how to keep it working mechanically. We were filled with gratitude for their help, yet daily we became more conscious of how little anyone really knew about caring for respiratory polio patients.

CHARLENE. My mother and father had been living in Lubbock for several months before Susan's illness while Daddy built a small house for us. Baptist churches in Texas cities, like those of other states, had pretty much gone out of the parsonage business. Arnett-Benson Baptist Church, where Cecil was pastor, was in the midst of a mushrooming community and had grown so rapidly that the church was hard pressed to keep up with providing space for all its activities.

Our church members were very concerned and supportive all during those hard first days. We were not the only members of Arnett-Benson Church facing this dire disease. Our custodian's daughter-in-law was also stricken with respiratory polio and put into an iron lung in a room right across the hall from Susan in the Lubbock hospital. However, she resisted the lung so strongly that it could not ventilate her properly, and she died. This, of course, was frightening to us as we watched Susan struggle with the lung.

Stella Herod, our church nursery worker, whose son had contracted polio a couple of years before Susan, understood, perhaps better than anyone, what we were going through. During those long uneasy days, Mrs. Herod came often to relieve me. She and Susan had been good friends as Susan often assisted her when the little ones in the nursery were crying. She always referred to Susan as "my little helper," and Susan felt secure with her. I learned later that the parents of small children in the church were panic-stricken when they learned Susan had polio. Susan had helped Mrs. Herod with the children during a funeral just the day before she became ill. Thankfully, no other children became ill.

3
Reliance on God

CECIL. From the moment we realized that Susan had polio, Charlene and I, joined by many friends, prayed for God's help—and His healing hand. Whenever there was time, we shared our prayer experiences with one another and drew strength from the sharing. For both of us, one night in particular stood out above all the others. I was out of town. While praying that night, I had what I understood to be an assurance from God that Susan would live. I felt at peace, sensing that somehow God was going to answer our prayers for Susan.

To tell the truth, I wasn't at all sure if it meant He was going to give us a miraculous healing. I didn't know what that experience meant, except that I believed God had a purpose for Susan. At the time, I may have read more into it than I now know was in His plan. That same night, Charlene had a similar experience, although we were six hundred miles apart. She called to tell me, not knowing what had happened with me. We both felt strongly that Susan would be all right, although we did not yet know what "all right" might mean.

I don't remember telling the church a lot of details, but I did share that I believed the Lord had assured us in some way that Susan would be all right. I didn't know what my experience meant and told them so, but it scared some of them. Several people questioned me—not chided—but questioned me as to what I meant. "You really staked out your faith," they said, but I knew that what happened that night to both of us was real. We could not explain it and did not understand it, but we took it as a promise of victory.

I've never gotten away from that, and the events that followed later—what Susan was eventually able to do compared to what she could do at that time—were as great a miracle as if she stood up and walked. Now, looking back through the unfolding years, I can see how dramatic and powerful was God's answer to our prayers.

Every day brought some new crisis for us during those days in the Lubbock hospital. Two frightening incidents related to the iron lung occurred in those early weeks—known as the "crisis time" of polio. The first came as a result of a tear in the rubber gasket that served as a collar that fitted around Susan's neck. The collar had to fit snugly to ensure the proper pressure was maintained within the tank, but it was torn slightly when Susan was first hurriedly put into the tank on Tuesday.

Little by little, the tear increased until, by early Sunday morning, it had reached the point where Susan was struggling for breath. Again, only the firemen knew how things worked, and even their knowledge was limited. We knew something must be done and done quickly, so we put in a call to the fire station for help. They responded immediately.

Charlene was still at home but just in the nick of time, my brother, Truett, from San Angelo, walked into the room. Not only did we need another pair of hands but having him with me gave me strength. Quickly, we assigned each person a task. We made sure everyone knew his assignment, the time in which it had to be done, and the order in which we had to move. One of the firemen was to help me with Susan, another was to be sure everything was clear inside the tank-bed for quickly putting Susan back in, another was to remove the right wing nut, and another was to remove the left wing nut holding the metal rim. These had to be removed speedily in order to loosen the metal rim which held the rubber gasket. Then we had to remove the torn collar and replace it with the new one, put the metal rim back on, then pull all five straps used to open the collar for Susan's head.

We knew Susan's life depended on our doing it fast and doing it right! As soon as the old collar was pulled open by the straps, I picked up Susan's limp body and hurried her to the bed where the firemen had a chest shell and respirator ready and running. We hurriedly laid the shell over Susan's small diaphragm and pressed it down so it would work. Unfortunately, it did not perform well. The whole operation took about ten minutes, but it seemed like an eternity. When everything was finally ready, the firemen lifted the shell away from Susan's chest, and I rushed across the room to place Susan in the tank. Again, everyone worked rapidly to get her in place, release the straps that sealed the collar, and close the tank.

At this point, I could see no evidence of life in Susan. She lay pale and still as a wax doll, with only her long pony tail and narrow little face showing as the giant metal tank continued to whoosh air in and out. Had we fixed the problem? Did we move fast enough? Were our efforts too little? too late? "Please, Lord," I prayed. "Don't let us lose her now. She's so small and so helpless. Please Lord, not now."

We stood there and searched fearfully for some sign of life. At first, there was nothing and I thought my heart would break. Then, gradually, a tiny bit of color began to creep into her face. We held our breaths as her expression changed, bit by bit, from china doll to little girl. Finally, she opened her eyes and smiled a little. God had answered my prayer. The time was not now.

When Susan could talk to us and assure us she was all right, I finally relaxed enough to thank Truett and the firemen for their help. I suddenly realized it was Sunday morning church time, and I had other responsibilities to fulfill. Charlene arrived. As I changed clothes, I quickly filled her in on what had occurred. Then Truett and I hurried off to church. Surprisingly enough, by the time we arrived, I had remembered most of my sermon. After reporting the crisis to the church and having a prayer of thanksgiving, the worship service went well. In spite of our doubts and fearful hearts, we were learning firsthand that the grace of God could meet all our needs.

The second crisis with Susan came a few days later. To us, at that point, every incident seemed a crisis. In many other ways, this incident was the most difficult. Charlene and I were both with Susan that day, although we usually took turns. Our doctor came in to check Susan and spent a good bit of time repeating the same procedure, over and over again. Finally, he turned to us and told us that Susan was not doing well. Susan had gotten much weaker, he said, and her heart was greatly stressed. He doubted she would live through the night.

We looked at one another in disbelief. Could we have misunderstood what we both thought were assurances from God that Susan would live to serve Him? We had been so sure of God's promise to give her not only life but abundant life! How could we have misunderstood so completely?

Charlene was frantic and did not want to leave us, but I insisted. I would stay with Susan as always and call her if there was any change. Little Lanny was waiting at home, and he needed some time with his mother, too. Even as Charlene left, I knew she had the harder part—not knowing from moment to moment what was happening or even if Susan was still alive. My heart was torn between my grieving wife and my dying child.

In the quiet hours of the night, I sat looking at Susan and the iron prison that kept her alive. It obviously wasn't providing enough of what she needed, but was the crisis in the machine itself, or was it in the small, frail body it housed? If the problem was in Susan, I could only pray for God to take over. If it was in the machine, then perhaps there was something we could do to make it work more efficiently.

Certainly, I knew very little at this time about this metal monster that ruled our lives, but the knack that God had given me to understand how things work began to kick in. I found myself thinking through the mechanical functions of the iron lung. Refusing to believe that God's promise to us had been wrongly perceived, I hastily prayed for insight as my mind began to hopscotch from one factor to another. I retraced in my mind all that I had seen the doctor and the firemen do in setting up the lung for Susan. Suddenly, I remembered that early that morning the doctor had readjusted the tank, reducing the negative pressure factor which I later came to know as the breath-intake function. Susan had grown steadily worse since that time.

I wasn't sure just why changing the negative pressure had caused the trouble, but I felt sure that was the answer. Alone in that room with my little dying daughter, I reached out to God with a plea for some way to help her. I did not fully understand how the tank worked, so I was hesitant to change anything, but Susan was in grave danger and I felt it was directly related to the way the tank operation was set. The doctor's dire warning that Susan probably would not live through the night pounded and pounded in my brain. My mouth was dry as dust, and my own heart was so heavy I could scarcely breathe.

With shaking hands, knowing the risk I was taking, but feeling it was her only chance, little by little I changed the tank setting, then took a deep breath and prayed. For hours afterward, I did not take my eyes off Susan, watching for any small sign that would tell me I had made a fatal mistake. Now I realize how simple it all is, but, at that time, I changed the gauges with fear and trembling. I had prayed, asking God for guidance. His answer was to give me a sense of peace in taking this action.

The next morning when the doctor came by, he was astonished at how well Susan was doing. She seemed stronger and more alert; all signs of heart stress were gone. For a moment I struggled with whether or not to tell him what I had done during that nightmare night when I had taken Susan's very life into my hands, but I decided to tell him exactly what I had done. He made no comment except to repeat that Susan was much better; what he may have said later to his colleagues about idiotic Baptist preachers, I have no way of knowing.

I soon learned that I could have helped Susan even more if I had known that changing not only the amount of pressure, but the number of breaths, was important. At that time, the machine was set to breathe at an adult rate, about sixteen breaths per minute. Four-year-old Susan, needing twenty-six to twenty-eight breaths per minute, was literally starving for oxygen. Though the art of polio-patient care was certainly not as developed as it would become over the next twenty years, this simple bit of information about the difference in breath-per-minute (bpm) rates for children and adults enabled me to assist two other very young children in similar crises by adjusting their iron lungs to twenty-eight bpm.

These critical experiences with Susan and others became part of God's education of Cecil and Charlene to better understand how to help Susan as well as others. The things they had learned became basic to the family's ability to keep Susan alive and give her joy and a reason for being. Knowing how helpless other parents must feel, and imagining how frightened the patients themselves must be, Cecil made it a priority to learn all he could about mechanical breathing aids. In the months ahead, two other polio victims in Lubbock faced similar crises. In each of these cases, the doctors urgently requested Cecil Ray and the firemen to help. By this time, Cecil had learned the secrets of making the chest shell work, and the doctors now recognized Cecil's understanding of the iron lung and how to set it to provide adequate breathing help.

CHARLENE. When the first critical stage of Susan's disease was over, the doctor started making arrangements for us to move Susan to another hospital since she was totally dependent on the iron lung. The place he found was the Southwestern Poliomyelitis Respiratory Center in Houston. So, after nearly five weeks in the Lubbock hospital, we began making plans to go to Houston.

We were eager to transfer Susan to Houston, but how? Friends—we never knew who or how many—worked with our U.S. Senator to provide a military plane from Brooke Field to take us, but we had no idea how the actual move would be accomplished. We had expected the plane to arrive at Reece Air Force Base around noon to take us; however, it was late afternoon when it finally arrived. The plane was accompanied by the doctor who had developed a portable tank respirator to bring polio-stricken servicemen home from overseas. He would handle the transport of Susan from one hospital to the other.

CECIL. My "pre-event" tension level was at its highest when we began to make plans to move Susan from the Lubbock hospital to Houston that first time. Although we had been assured that the doctor and equipment were the best the world could offer, up to this point we had not worked with anyone who totally understood Susan's condition, knew how to cope with the situation, and fully knew how to operate tank respirators, so I had little feel as to what "the best the world could offer" might mean. I expressed my concerns to the Air Force doctor who would accompany us and asked to see the equipment Susan would be using. We drove out to

Reece Air Force Base, and he patiently showed me the equipment and its position in the plane, thus relieving my fears. I realized with great relief that, for the first time, we would be in the hands of someone who really understood and knew how to care for Susan. If he was impatient with me for my questions and concerns, he did not show it. We took the portable unit from the plane and returned to the hospital for Charlene and Susan.

CHARLENE. It was dark when Cecil and the doctor with his portable tank came rushing back in. The transfer from the big Emerson iron lung to the portable one was done quickly. We all crowded into the waiting ambulance, rushed to the airport, into the military plane, and away into the night sky. Susan was wide-eyed at all the activity and at the very idea that she was flying high above the Texas clouds.

The doctor was a specialist at caring for victims of polio and took complete charge of Susan. Soon, the lights of Houston were below us and the plane settled down on the runway. Then there was another transfer from the plane to an ambulance which whisked us into Houston and the hospital there. They were expecting us. A team of nurses came running out, and we just stood and watched in wonder as utter efficiency took over. What a relief to see they knew exactly what to do for Susan! I drew a deep, deep breath of relief and thanked God.

Into the darkened hospital where all the other patients were asleep. Down the hall with sounds of many iron lungs going "whew-whoosh," "whew-whoosh," "whew-whoosh" in the night. Into the children's ward where another big Emerson tank was open and waiting for her. Here Susan would be safe.

By the time she was settled in, all the other children were awake. Susan looked around at them through the rearview mirror of the tank above her head. These children were to be her wardmates and hopefully her new friends. She was not alone in having to live in an iron lung. A little smile played around her mouth, saying, "I think I'll like it here." Cecil and I breathed a sigh of relief. We had come to the right place.

CECIL. With a little nudge from the head nurse and assurances to Susan that we would be close by, Charlene and I went out to the waiting room and settled down on two of the sofas to catch a few winks until morning. We were exhausted both physically and emotionally. I remember trying to make a call to let someone back home know we had arrived safely. I started putting money into the phone slot and woke up as the coins hit the floor with a clatter. I don't even remember if I ever finished that call.

We knew many of our friends, and many others who knew of our situation from news sources, were praying for us. The future still hung, like an unknown cloud, over every facet of our lives; but, for the first time in almost two months, we began to feel some measure of security. The doctors and medical staff here knew what they were doing.

Next day, one of my cousins who lived in Houston took us to a nearby motel where we waited until my parents came with Lanny. In the meantime, our family, although scattered across the state, knew of our safe arrival from the news reports in the papers and on television. My mother learned, as she attended her Woman's Missionary Union (WMU) meeting, from a friend who was watching the news faithfully. It seems Susan's plight had caught the imagination and interest of people all over Texas, and the status of her condition was reported regularly.

After Susan and Charlene were settled in, I went back to Lubbock to resume the task of pastoring the church there, while Charlene, Lanny, and Charlene's parents settled in a Houston apartment for an indefinite stay. The months to come would be both a test and an affirmation of God's continuing answer to prayer.

Although I was living in Lubbock, my heart was with my family. I made a number of trips back to Houston. On my first trip back, I took Charlene a Ford coupe to use while there. On the way, I swung by Greenville, Texas, to perform the marriage of James and Virginia Clark. James was a close friend of ours, having attended Arnett-Benson Church before going to Wayland College. Through the years, a close friendship has existed between our families. James went to Nashville upon his graduation and marriage to work at the Sunday School Board, where he spent his entire career, working at every level, finally serving as executive vice-president with Grady Cothen.

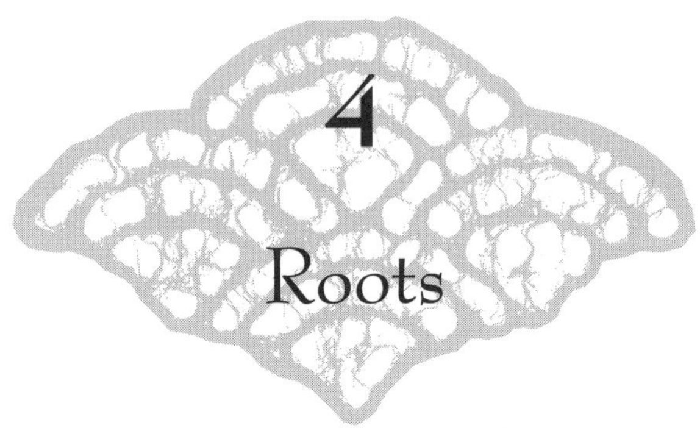

Roots

Cecil and Charlene were focused on a plan for their lives from the beginning. They would serve Christ through their ministry and through the witness of their everyday lives. For Charlene, missions and mission support were of prime importance, and she resolved to encourage interest and support through emphasizing missions in every area of the church's programs.

They met as teenagers in 1939 when Cecil came from Llano, Texas, to live with his brother and sister-in-law, Truett and Lois Ray. He was to attend San Angelo Junior College on a football scholarship. Cecil had graduated from high school at age sixteen, partly because he had skipped a grade and partly because of when his birthday fell.

The son of a Baptist minister, Cecil had lived in San Angelo as a boy when his father served as pastor of Immanuel Baptist Church and as director of missions for the Concho Valley Baptist Association. He accepted Christ at age seven and was licensed to preach at age seventeen by Immanuel Church. Joye Charlene was born on a Texas ranch, the only child of Ida and Charlie Andrews. Her mother was a homemaker and her father a building contractor. He built two of the homes Cecil and Charlene lived in during their early Texas years. Charlene was a good student and excelled in school activities. She was valedictorian of her senior class. She was a junior in high school when she met Cecil the Christmas before she was seventeen. They hit it off from the start. On the night of her graduation from high school, Cecil proposed and Charlene accepted. Although young, they had a clear vision of the purpose and direction for their lives together: they would honor God in every area of their lives. Now, more than fifty-five years later, this is still the thrust of their lives.

In 1940, Cecil moved to Brownwood to attend Howard Payne College. Charlene followed in the fall of 1941 and received her engagement ring from Cecil her first week of college. She and Cecil were married in June 1942. They were each nineteen years old.

CHARLENE. Our first two months were spent in a tiny apartment in Rowena, near Ballinger, Texas. In the fall, we moved to Dale, near Winters, Texas, where Cecil was principal and teacher in a three-teacher school. Cecil also served as pastor of both Hatchell and Rowena Baptist Churches. During the summer of 1943, we attended Southwestern Baptist Theological Seminary in Fort Worth. Cecil had finished Howard Payne College but had to get special permission to attend seminary because they required students to be twenty-two years of age at enrollment. Since I did not intend to graduate, I was given special permission to take classes even though I was only twenty and had not completed college.

CECIL. In the fall of 1943, Charlene and I moved to Gruenwald where I was principal and both of us taught in the same small school. Charlene taught grades one through four, and I taught grades five through eight. We had taken correspondence courses from Howard Payne College which allowed us to get teachers' certificates. I continued to serve as pastor of Rowena Church as well.

In the summer of 1944, we moved to Fort Worth to attend Southwestern Seminary full-time. We found a nice little house with one bedroom, a tiny living room, and a kitchen. During 1944–1945, we served the church at Alexander, near Dublin, where I challenged the church to undertake a building program. The church voted to build and desperately needed to build, but was not really dedicated to the task. Later, they told me that every pastor before me had also insisted they build but did not follow through. At first, they did not take me seriously either—that is until I led the church to vote to tear down the old building so we could use the materials in building a new one. Now it was build or else!

Next day, after voting in favor of my plan, a crew of church members I had enlisted came prepared for the task. We worked until late evening. Before we left, we had completely torn down the old building and were cleaning and sorting the materials for reuse. For the first time, members realized they were really going to build.

In 1946, Cecil was called to pastor Arnett-Benson Baptist Church in Lubbock, and he and Charlene moved into a little house nearby. This church had begun as a mission of Calvary Baptist Church of Lubbock, but within weeks of its formation, Sunday School attendance at the

*mission had reached 180. In just under a year, Arnett-Benson was orga-
nized into a church and began a building program. Their first task
included jacking up the existing small building, turning it around,
digging a half-basement beside it, then lifting the building up and over
and setting it down on top of the basement. It also involved buying the
house next door. These were busy days for Cecil and Charlene as they
helped guide the new church's growth and awaited the birth of their first
child. As Cecil led the church in building its physical facilities and its
membership, Charlene worked to build WMU programs and to develop
the church's mission vision and involvement. It was into this climate of
exciting commitment and service that little Susan Ray was born on July
14, 1948. She was a bright and happy child, healthy and active until the
day she was stricken.*

*The 1952 polio epidemic was raging. The Southwestern Poliomyelitis
Respiratory Center in Houston was crowded beyond capacity. Every day
more patients were admitted; by far the largest number of them were
children. The doctors and nurses were exhausted, and space was a
forgotten luxury, but it was a welcome haven to Cecil and Charlene Ray.*

*In laboratories all across the world, scientists and their assistants
worked frantically to protect the populace against the horror, and fear
made captives of families all across this nation.*

5
Logistics, Learning, and Love

CHARLENE. When we had Susan settled in at the hospital in Houston, we found a small apartment nearby. My parents came to stay with me, to keep little Lanny, and to help make life for us as normal as it could be under the circumstances. Cecil and I have never forgotten the great sacrifice in income and convenience they made then in order to help us, because, as you might imagine, a builder doesn't get paid unless he works. To be honest, I don't see how we could have ever managed without their help.

I could only visit Susan on Wednesday and Sunday afternoons. There simply wasn't space for visitors, even immediate family. They did, however, permit Cecil to visit her whenever he could come to Houston. After a time, the nurse told me Susan was hardly eating anything. She was getting weaker and the doctor thought she needed a blood transfusion. Friends we had made at South Main Street Baptist Church gave blood for her, and Susan began to perk up a bit, but she still would eat almost nothing. She wanted some "pigs-in-a blanket" and little green lima beans. The doctor encouraged me to fix and bring her some. I began going to the hospital every evening at suppertime and feeding Susan her "pigs" and limas and anything else she wanted.

CECIL. I recall one very scary experience during Susan's early weeks at the hospital. I had flown in from Lubbock for a visit, and Charlene and I had gone shopping for a few things to brighten Susan's life. As you might imagine, we always made sure the hospital and Charlene's parents knew where we were at all times. We were in a nearby store, choosing hair bows for her ponytail, when Charlene's father came rushing in to tell us the doctor had called. There was an emergency with Susan, and we were needed back at the hospital as soon as possible

We simply left a surprised clerk holding the things we had selected and dashed back to the hospital. It was a twenty-minute drive, and before we could get there, we had dealt with every probability and fear the human heart can know. Once again, we searched our hearts. Had we misunderstood God's purpose for Susan's life? Had all our hopes been built on merely wishful thinking rather than a sure promise from God?

By the time we arrived at the hospital, the crisis was over and Susan was out of danger. The crisis involved an attempt to have Susan use a rocking bed, a device they believed would assist her in breathing. It was the first time they had tried this procedure, and she had panicked, and so had not responded well at all. We were told that she should not attempt this again, but later, at home, we tried and were finally successful in having her use this procedure.

It is hard for us today to imagine what life was like for Susan and the other children who lived out their days in iron lungs. Trapped in a huge metal monstrosity that sucked and whooshed noisily, they could not use their hands to play, could barely see one another through the rearview mirrors mounted on the tanks over their heads, and could scarcely hear one another for the breathing noises the machines made.

Try not scratching your nose, or even blowing it after a sneeze. Sit with your hands idle while your eyelid twitches or your head is chinked to one side. Add to that being able to see your parents only twice a week. Is it any wonder that many of these small victims gave up and quit fighting?

CHARLENE. During those nightly visits to feed Susan in the children's ward, I saw how shorthanded the center was. I began doing small things for the other children: helping to feed them, moving arms and legs to a more comfortable position, scratching noses, or pulling their tanks around so they could see someone better. Finally, I asked the head nurse if I could come in every day to help out. This was before the concept of volunteerism had come about, but the nurses and aides all seemed relieved to have someone else helping in the children's ward, so I began putting in about eight to ten hours a day, trying to keep the children halfway satisfied. Their entire world was composed of iron lungs, chest shells, and rocking beds, and life held little fun or pleasure for them. Of course, it was because I had my parents there in Houston to help me with Lanny that I was able to help out at all.

Cecil's parents also came to see Susan while she was in Houston. It was their first time to see her since she was stricken. Unfortunately, this first visit was on one of Susan's not-so-good days—she was upset and not doing well at all. Seeing her this way on their first visit was very difficult, for Cecil and me, and for them as well. Fortunately, they were able to visit her again before they left Houston. This time, Susan was happy and could enjoy their visit.

Susan, of course, was delighted that her mother could be with her every day, but, young as she was, she remembered her little brother, Lanny, and reminded her mother to take time out to play with him and take him to the park.

Now, in looking back on the Houston experience, it is easy to see how God, even then, was preparing Charlene for the role she would assume in Susan's care and education in the years to come. He was also molding Susan as she learned to be patient with her limitations and to be thoughtful of others. This characteristic of thoughtfulness was apparent to everyone who spent time with Susan and was one of her most endearing traits. It was during these long hard weeks when she was first confined to the tank that she developed the sunny disposition which drew people to her for the rest of her life.

CHARLENE. Susan had been in Houston for several weeks and seemed to be making little improvement from the standpoint of gaining strength or of regaining any movement. On top of everything else, she had a bad throat infection. One night, when all the children were sleeping, I laid my head on my arms and wept as I prayed, "Dear Lord, if you will let Susan live, we will do our best to rear her as a person somehow useful in your service, and if it is to be, please give us a sign." When I finished my prayer, it felt as if God had not heard, for nothing seemed changed. I left to go home with a heavy heart.

The next day, when I went into Susan's ward, a nurse met me with excitement. "Come see what Susan can do!" she cried. I peered through the window of the tank, and Susan was just barely moving her right leg! This was the first movement of any kind she had made and the sign I had prayed for! I called Cecil to tell him and found he had also had a very similar experience. We knew once again that Susan would live and that God had a plan for her—a way for her to serve.

That same week, the 20 June 1952 issue of the Arnett-Benson **Baptist Visitor** *contained a brief report to the congregation from pastor Cecil Ray:*

> Last night, after church, I talked with Mrs. Ray and also wished her a
> happy anniversary (our tenth). She tells me that Susan has had a pretty
> bad week. A throat infection set her back some, but, now that she is
> better, she is being allowed out of the lung and into the chest respirator
> for an hour in the morning and an hour in the afternoon.

The doctors report that no improvement in her breathing can be detected. The only improvement recently has been a slight gain in the movement of her right arm and leg. We would desire that you continue to pray for us.

CHARLENE. As summer progressed, the epidemic grew worse. Some days, as many as ten new patients were brought into the hospital. Susan had been at the center for four months but still was unable to breathe on her own. The doctors were kind and concerned, of course, but could not promise any improvement. Our best hope was to rely on the prayer assurances that Cecil and I had been given.

America had rallied wholeheartedly behind efforts to conquer polio. President Franklin D. Roosevelt, a polio victim himself, had founded the National Foundation for Infantile Paralysis in 1938. He had enlisted Basil O'Connor, his former law partner and trusted friend, to head up this foundation as president and to lead efforts to conquer the disease.

The next decade brought little progress until a major breakthrough occurred in 1949 when Harvard scientists, Drs. Frederick Robins, John Endears, and Thomas Welder, were able, for the first time, to grow the polio virus in test tube cultures. This provided a practical means of replicating viruses for research and hopefully for making a vaccine.

Research supported through the annual March of Dimes had enabled scientists to identify more than one hundred strains of polio viruses. Now they confronted a crucial next step: could these various strains be segregated into types? This was essential if a vaccine to protect against all strains was to be developed. A thirty-three-year-old scientist, Dr. Jonas Salk, had been selected to head the laboratory at the University of Pittsburgh, and was having some success in overcoming this problem. By 1951, the year before Susan was stricken, Salk was able to announce that the strains had been separated into three types. It was the breakthrough they had been waiting for. It finally appeared that a vaccine could be designed to halt the scourge!

CHARLENE. Soon after Susan's birthday in July, Dr. Pfeiffer told us she was going to have to send some patients home.

"We simply must have more space to care for all the new patients that are pouring in," she said. "We have never sent anyone home before who was not weaned from the tank, but Susan can tolerate the shell respirator for a time and, with your experience here at the hospital, I believe you folk can learn to manage at home."

Home! What a happy, frightening thought!

"How long do you think Susan can live?" I asked.

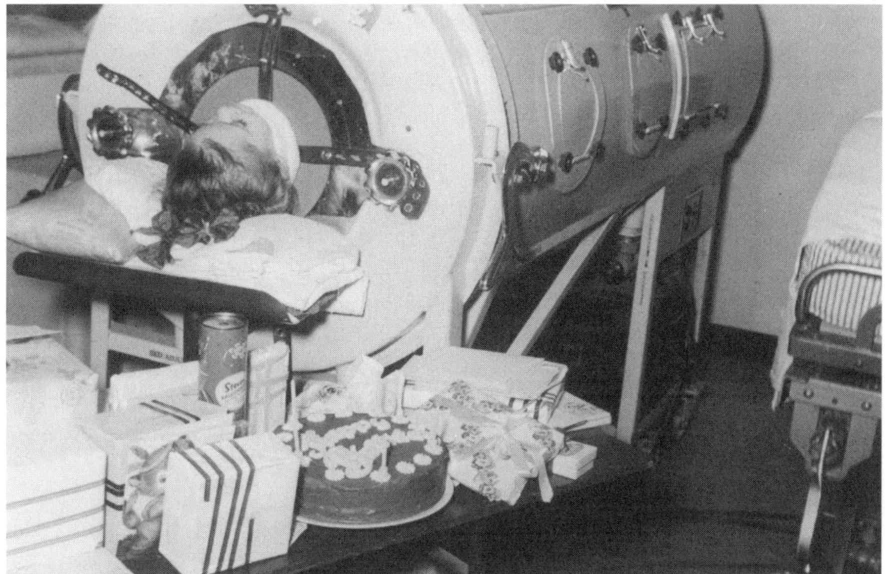

Susan's fifth birthday, in Houston.

Dr. Pfeiffer replied, "Oh, three to six months, probably."

My heart sank. Only six months at best. Such a little time to have our precious daughter!

Again, I remembered how Cecil and I had both felt God's promise that Susan would live to serve Him. We knew He is faithful and filled with compassion. Now we would need to trust Him to fulfill His promise even in the face of all that medicine could predict. We had trusted our child to medical science, and it had served her well thus far, but we remembered the faithfulness God had shown us again and again, through even the darkest hours. Somehow we knew that God had a better future for this child, but could not have imagined how He would bring it to pass.

When the doctor left, I called Cecil in Lubbock; we began the task of making arrangements to go home.

CECIL. When we learned that Susan was to come home, we started counting the days. Our delight in having our family all together again outweighed the fears of what we might face. Sure, we had been told that Susan likely would not live beyond six months, but we were so involved in making plans for her homecoming, I'm not sure we ever really accepted the doctor's prediction. Together, and in our own home. This made every little thing we planned seem important and gave each day special meaning. Every improvement we saw in Susan—even slight ones—gave us encouragement. Needless to say, Susan could hardly wait.

Susan had gone to Houston in a military plane, attended by the physician who had designed the special transport lung for the Air Force. Coming home she was transported in a U.S. Air Force cargo plane, a C-54. She was still in the big Emerson tank she had been in while at the Houston center. Since the plane was designed for cargo, her respirator was set in the center of the cargo area and securely bolted to the floor. A few passenger seats in the front of the plane provided seats for Charlene and me and some of the attending Air Force personnel. Susan remained in the large tank respirator even after she was settled in the living room of our little Lubbock house on Second Street. Even though we had seen her homecoming as a glorious victory, as life at home with Susan and her special needs began, we faced a number of problems to be overcome. However, as each potential crisis surfaced, it seemed God had an answer or an alternate route ready for us.

The first problem we faced was the fact that our little house could not hold all of Susan's equipment. Even though Arnett-Benson Church was struggling to provide enough space to accommodate its rapid increase in members, still some of the men got busy and began construction on a larger house for us. Another big problem we anticipated was how we would cope in the event of an electrical power failure since Susan's respirator depended on electricity to operate. Lubbock was a rare city in that all residents had the choice of two power companies. Each company had its own lines in alleys back of the houses, and residents chose the service they preferred. In our case, the answer lay in subscribing to both services. In this way, should one service fail, we could switch to the alternate service.

Members of our church rallied to the need immediately. They provided us with a large automatic switch that would instantly shift our house current from one electrical service to another in case of power failure. The switchover was so fast we were never aware of the change unless one of us was looking at a light at that moment. Then we might detect a slight flicker. This same service was transferred to the new pastorium when we moved in December 1952. Lubbock was the only city where we had this double-service option. During those first critical years, not having to deal with an electrical outage was a blessing indeed.

At first, I would not accept any out-of-town engagements, but by the end of February, Susan was doing so much better that I gradually accepted some meetings away. I was fortunate that I had been able to continue as full-time pastor of our church with the many responsibilities that involved, but Charlene was temporarily forced to give up her efforts on behalf of mission education and promotion so she could care for Susan. Later, she was able to resume these tasks, which pleased us both very much. I had come to depend on her enthusiasm and ideas to undergird and enrich my own ministry.

CHARLENE. It took a moving van to take us from the Lubbock airport to our little house when we returned from Houston that first time. Mother, Daddy, and little Lanny were there waiting for us. Oh, it was so good to be home. It took some doing, but that giant Emerson tank was finally maneuvered into the small living room. It simply would not fit in any of our other rooms. Our sofa opened into a bed where I slept one night and Cecil the next. My parents stayed on with us for a short time, then moved to an apartment in Lubbock until the next fall. Seeing then that we were managing well in caring for Susan, they went back to their home in San Angelo. When I think back over the years, I see that we could never have managed to stay with Susan during those first months in Houston or gotten along as well during those first days back home had it not been for the loving sacrifice my parents made in setting aside their own lives to give us a hand.

CECIL. Much of Susan's life story is an account of overcoming barriers and limitations. At first, she was limited to the living-dining room of that little house in Lubbock. We arranged the room to accommodate her tank, so she ate, slept, and spent every day there. The tank was about nine feet long when closed. Open, it required nearly seventeen feet of space.

Our first effort to enlarge Susan's world, and also my first attempt at building equipment for her, was a child-sized version of the large reclining chair she had used occasionally at the center in Houston. While in it, she used her chest respirator. This small chair I made was fitted to her dimensions; with it, she was able to go into "her" room. With help from family and friends, she could play with her dolls, her little table and chairs, and her dishes. Someone had to move these toys for her, of course, but she took great delight in giving directions and having them acted out by others. This was the beginning of a long list of chairs (see Appendix: Susan's "Enablers"), each one designed to help Susan at a given time, for a given need.

CHARLENE. Dr. Pfeiffer had tried to get Susan to use the rocking bed while we were in Houston but without success. The bed was simply a hospital-type bed that rocked up and down, end to end. It was a very minimal breathing aid that worked with gravity to move the patient's diaphragm up and down, to force air in and out, but Susan had not been able to tolerate it at all. She had panicked and almost died while using one in Houston that day we were buying ribbons for her hair, and the doctors had determined that it would not be safe for her to use it. Nevertheless, Cecil was determined that Susan should have another go at it since its use was considered at that time to be a step toward breathing recovery.

CECIL. I felt strongly that Susan could benefit from the use of a rocking bed; however, we did not have a doctor's prescription for one, which meant neither our insurance nor the March of Dimes would help provide one. Like all of the medical equipment Susan needed through the years, the rocking beds were expensive. The one I made cost only about fifty dollars, and it worked quite well.

This factor proved true in regard to nearly every piece of equipment that we had for Susan; because I could build it, we did not have to have a doctor's prescription for it. We never thought of this approach to making or securing equipment for Susan ourselves as any lack of respect for her doctors. Rather, it was a way for us to help Susan and to make it possible for her to do things that otherwise she could not do. This, too, was part of the way God enabled her to serve Him.

To build her rocking bed, I located an old hospital bed and enlisted the help of Homer Allred, a church member and good friend. I located and cut metal pieces and Homer welded them for me. Together, we put a rocking arm and electric motor underneath the bed. It operated like a bed seesaw, using the natural gravity principle to help Susan breathe. As her head came up, her diaphragm tended to fall, thus creating an inhale breath. As the bed rocked back, it produced the opposite—an exhale breath. This was also my first attempt at finding the correct pulleys and belts so I could reduce the motor's seventeen hundred rpms to allow about twenty-six rocks per minute, which was Susan's breath rate at that time.

When the bed was complete, we hauled it to our house. We were aware of what had happened before and thus very cautious in having Susan try it out. The first day, Susan was able to tolerate it only for a minute or two before we had to rush her back into the tank. This became a daily attempt, and very little progress was made. She was simply terrified at being outside her lung. But we kept trying, and with Charlene using puppets and stories to distract her, Susan could finally manage about ten minutes at a time.

On the sixtieth day we tried, Franklin Swanner, a preacher friend of mine who was district director of Baptist work in our area, came for a visit. Susan knew Franklin well and delighted in his teasing her. He began his usual tomfoolery, and Susan was so caught up in it she forgot her fear. Before we realized it, she had been breathing on the rocking bed for forty-five minutes! Beginning with that breakthrough, Susan increased her time until she eventually rocked for at least an hour, twice a day. The rocking bed provided a welcome change from the big tank in which she spent most of her time. The number of breaths per minute was first set at twenty-nine; however, over the years, it gradually decreased as she matured. During the last twenty years of her life, Susan breathed at about twelve breaths per minute.

Arnett-Benson was still enjoying phenomenal growth, with a Sunday School attendance of over six hundred. The congregation had recently completed a new sanctuary and educational space and now turned their full attention to the larger house they were building for Susan and her family.

Building a specially designed house for a little girl who could not exist without help to breathe was of great interest to the people of Texas and became the subject of several newspaper articles. The **Baptist Standard,** *the Texas Baptist state newspaper, gave such publicity that people from all over Texas sent money to help build it. Susan had captured the hearts of people all across the state.*

CHARLENE. It was a beautiful, dark-red, brick house with three bedrooms, two baths, a large living-dining room, kitchen with a breakfast nook, and a big, big room for Susan. It even had central heating and cooling. Neither Cecil nor I had ever lived in such a house before. Susan missed her little friends from Second Street when we first moved, but there were church children nearby who came to visit and play with her, and she soon felt very much at home.

LANNY. My memory kicks in about the time we moved into the new pastorium. For me, it was simply a given that our home was filled with all this equipment. That was the way the world normally was for me. Thinking back, now that I have kids of my own, I realize that we just took for granted all the equipment necessary to keep Susan alive and well. It was later on that I realized not everybody had someone in the household who needed such specialized equipment and care.

Today, we would be horrified at the electrical and mechanical hazards we lived with: the moving parts going up and down with exposed belts and pulleys in which a child could get a hand or a finger caught. Nowadays, lawyers and insurance people would be horrified, but I grew up with them and thought nothing of it.

One of the things I do remember quite vividly was Susan's giant Emerson tank. When I was a small child, that tank seemed enormous— filling the room. My mother always worried that I would get caught in the big mechanical arm that caused the bellows to breathe back and forth, but she needn't have worried. I was terrified of it and never got too close. In fact, I never got hurt on any of Susan's equipment except for a cut foot when I stepped on a small piece of metal off one of her chairs.

Aware of the financial burden communities were bearing in helping care for polio patients, monies collected through the March of Dimes began to be divided, with individual communities receiving half of what they had raised. The other half went into research and to educate and train medical and rehabilitation personnel.

For the Ray family, as for thousands of others, assistance with daily living was a godsend. Providing Susan's Emerson tank was the first assistance they gave. Then, upon their move into the new house in Lubbock, the March of Dimes provided the Rays with a live-in assistant who helped Charlene with Susan's care as well as with the cooking and cleaning chores.

CHARLENE. "Oh! That hurts!" I heard Susan complaining as Mrs. Byers, her physical therapist, stretched the tightening muscles in her left leg. But then Mrs. Byers began to sing in her slight but delightful Scottish brogue:

> If you knew Susie, like I know Susie
> Oh! Oh! Oh! what a girl!
> There's none so classy as that fair lassie,
> Oh! Oh! Oh, what a girl!

I peeked around the corner and saw Susan swinging her leg with Mrs. Byers's help, no longer complaining but eager to continue. With that one happy little song, Mrs. Byers helped Susan through the long, often painful therapy sessions that kept her arms and legs straight and warded off the twisted and contorted limbs that sometimes occur with paralysis. It was with the assistance of dedicated people such as Mrs. Byers that we were able to cope during those early years as over and over again, God met our needs through the kindness and dedication of people He sent into our lives.

6

To Everyone He Gives a Gift

CHARLENE. Now that Susan's therapy was progressing so well, I had only one other major concern. Susan had developed an unusual habit—she seemed to be swallowing air in large gulps, and I worried that she might choke or weaken the muscles in her diaphragm even further.

CECIL. In the early months after Susan returned from Houston that first time, there were two incidents involving other polio victims that also involved us. One night as I returned from preaching in a revival meeting, I learned that two-year-old Gregory Hannabus had been admitted to a Lubbock hospital and was in an iron lung. Although it was late, I went to the hospital, met the family, and learned that Gregory had undergone a tracheotomy but needed an attachment that would hold the collar of the lung away from the trach where it entered the throat.

Knowing something of the anxiety and fear Gregory's parents were feeling, I agreed to attempt to build an attachment and to have it ready the next day when their doctor was ready to install it. By this time, I had learned a great deal more than when we faced the crisis with Susan and her collar-changing experience. After talking with the doctor by phone, I learned that although he had a good sense of what was involved, he had no previous experience with this procedure. I carried the attachment I had built, along with Susan's Huxley respirator, and alerted the firemen of the need for a chest shell. This time the chest shell worked, and Gregory remained alert throughout the process.

This was the beginning of a friendship with the Hannabus family, and when the center in Houston, where Susan had been, finally had room for Gregory, we used the small tank respirator I had built for Susan earlier and transported Gregory to Houston in our car which we had redesigned so the side doors could open without a center post. This gave us room for any equipment we might need for traveling. In preparation for this trip, I also built Gregory a small twelve-volt dc aspirator since he frequently had need of one. He also required oxygen, so we designed attachments to accommodate a large oxygen bottle as well. Gregory made the long trip fine.

Some seven months later, I again provided transportation for his return to Lubbock. Gregory lived for one more year, and just two days before Christmas, I joined his Methodist pastor in conducting his funeral. It was a sad time for all of us and served to remind us afresh that life was fragile for these little ones who struggled with the effects of polio.

The second experience in which I was able to share what I had learned began with a call from Dr. Jenkins, who had been Susan's doctor when she first took polio. He called, asking if I could prepare a trach attachment for a small infant who had just contracted the disease. I fashioned one as quickly as possible—working into the night. Next day, I took the attachment to the hospital and learned that another dire emergency made it impossible for the doctor to be present for the procedure. The young parents were terrified, having no idea what to expect. They seemed to look to me for help, when, in truth, I felt as helpless as they. The nurse needed assistance though, and it appeared I was the only help available.

The baby was in isolation, so I donned a robe and mask to enter. I helped the nurse fit the chest shell around the baby's tiny diaphragm and lift him out of the tank. She installed the trach attachment and we put the baby back into the iron lung, holding our breaths as well. All during the procedure, I was aware that the child was almost as white as his sheets— just like Susan had been during her early crisis. He remained pale and limp even after we placed him back in the tank. I had not had time to check the tank setting until we had finished with the attachment, but I now found the tank was set at sixteen breaths per minute, an adult rate. The breath capacity was also too low. I called the nurse's attention to these settings, but she declared she was not allowed to change the setting unless the doctor instructed her to. She left the room for a moment to get supplies, and I explained to the parents that I had learned, through my own experience with Susan, that children needed more breaths per minute than adults. Although they knew I was no doctor, they seemed to trust me, so with their permission, I adjusted the baby's tank setting to twenty-eight to twenty-nine bpm and increased the breath capacity as well. By the time the nurse returned, the baby was beginning to show color in his face and signs of regaining consciousness. The nurse noticed this immediately. I then explained to her what I had done and why it was essential. I assured her I had already explained to the parents and had their consent. The baby continued to improve.

This family was from out of town, and I never saw them again. I was delighted to read in the paper two weeks later that the baby was well and being released from the hospital.

CHARLENE. After we had been back home for almost a year, we felt the need to return to the Houston hospital for a checkup for Susan. But how could we get there? Certainly we could not expect another military plane this time, and I knew there would be other times that we would need to transport Susan as well. Since Cecil had already begun his equipment building with a small lawn chair on wheels for everyday use and a small rocking chair to replace the big bed rocker, I asked, "Why don't you just build Susan a small tank to travel in?" Like most wives, it was easier for me to think up solutions than to carry them out, but I knew Cecil could come up with an answer if he put his mind to it.

CECIL. My brain started clicking. In a short time, I had thought it through and told Charlene I believed I could do it. The local sheet metal shop could build the body, and Manuel Shaffer could help me with the motors and bellows. I decided to give it a try.

We built the respirator with both ac and dc power systems so it could be powered while in the car. It was designed like the Drynker-Collins model which had bellows underneath the tank body, rather than at the back end like the Emerson lung. This made the unit shorter, thus taking up less space.

CHARLENE. When the new tank was finished, Cecil brought it home to try it out; but it was unpainted, welded-looking, and motley. Susan would have nothing to do with it. That tank took a quick trip to friend Fred Gentry's and came back a beautiful shade of pink. Susan took one look at it and approved. We placed her inside and stepped back, holding our breaths. It worked! Susan decided to name this smaller tank "Baby," and Baby it was for the rest of her life. Later, this same tank was painted white with gold rose decals to match her French Provincial furniture. It was still in use over forty years later at the time of her death.

CECIL. Susan spent the night in her new pink tank. She loved it and that night was a good test of its capacity to keep her comfortable. The next morning at 5:00 A.M., we began our pioneer trip back to Houston, packed in our 1935 wood-panel station wagon, and pulling a small borrowed trailer which contained her reclining chair and her small rocking chair.

CHARLENE. The trip to Houston was going nicely when, suddenly, Baby stopped working!

"What have we done?" I thought. "How could we believe we could travel with a child who cannot even breathe on her own? Susan will die, and it will be our fault!" Cecil pulled off the road as quickly as possible. All of us were panic-stricken at the thought that Susan could live for only a few minutes without air.

"Please help us, Lord," I prayed. My mind darted from fear to fear as we touched and tested every connection. Then, praise God, I discovered that my knee had accidentally hit the switch on the side of the tank and knocked the unit off. I clicked it back on and the unit began to purr again, pumping air into Susan's body as well as relief to our hearts. We resumed our journey, thankful to have discovered the source of the trouble so quickly and even more thankful that the solution was such a simple one. Maybe our efforts to give our family a fairly normal life were going to work after all.

CECIL. We were expected by the hospital in Houston, but we had not indicated how we would manage the trip. At that time, the only known methods of travel for those confined to an iron lung included chartering a large airplane, contracting with the railroad for use of a baggage car, or leasing a moving van. When we arrived at the hospital, we unloaded Baby with Susan in it, set a car battery under the unit to operate the tank, and rolled Susan into the hospital and down the hall. Shock and surprise registered on the faces of the staff as we admitted Susan for her checkup, and we were understandably delighted at their reaction.

CHARLENE. When Dr. Pfeiffer met us, she said, "Susan, you look great, but your parents look awful." Doubtless, our fright at having her unit stop running had left us slightly haggard. As Dr. Pfeiffer prepared to examine Susan, I confessed. "Doctor, I'm afraid I've allowed Susan to develop a very bad habit. I often find her doing something kind of funny—like smacking her lips or gulping air."

When we lifted Susan out of her tank, the doctor observed what I was talking about. "Praise the Lord," Dr. Pfeiffer said. "This five-year-old has learned for herself what I spend hours trying to teach adults to do. She's 'frogging!'" It was easy to see that Dr. Pfeiffer was delighted. It seems Susan had learned, perhaps of necessity, to swallow air as a frog does. This would eventually enable her to speak and to function with only minimal breathing assistance for nearly two hours. However, we were cautioned that to overdo this might be harmful. Her checkup showed she was progressing well. During her stay in Houston, Susan was allowed to remain in Baby rather than be placed in the larger hospital unit.

CECIL. Although Charlene had scolded Susan for what she thought was a bad habit, Susan had developed this technique of "frog-breathing" on her own. We had feared it would interfere with her developing an increased use of her chest muscles; instead, it proved to be an unexpected blessing. Charlene and I had prayed to God to give us a miracle—one that would open up a full and meaningful life for Susan. We had both felt a real assurance that God would respond to our prayers, but we were slow to realize that this new ability to "frog-breathe" was God's answer. In time, we would come to see that this one gift would open up the world to Susan in ways we could never have foreseen.

CHARLENE. Now we can look back and recognize the miracle that we and a host of friends had prayed for. Little by little, we understood that God did perform a miracle that enabled Susan to live beyond the possible and enjoy a rich fulfillment. Even today, we continue to marvel at what He enabled her to accomplish.

We had, however, another frightening experience soon after our initial Houston checkup. Dr. Miller, who was Susan's regular doctor, was out of town, and the doctor covering for her knew little about respiratory polio. We were still not as experienced in caring for Susan as we would be later, and this unexpected illness was terrifying. At first, we did not know where to turn, but we remembered that Dr. James Fannin, who was physician to the rest of our family, had shown a great deal of interest in Susan and her treatment, so we called and he came over. After checking her carefully, he returned to his office for an aspirator, came back and sat with her, finally spending the night by her bedside. The next morning, Dr. Fannin saw that Susan needed a level of care he was not trained for, so he recommended that we go back to the center in Houston. He called and canceled his appointments for the day and made preparations to go with us to Houston.

We set out in two cars, Susan, Cecil, Lanny, and I in one car, followed by Dr. Fannin and Waylon Edwards, his pastor and a dear friend of ours, in the second car. Seeing that Dr. Fannin had asked his pastor to go along made me uneasy. I wondered if he thought Susan might not survive the trip. Each time we stopped, Dr. Fannin would check Susan carefully. When we stopped to eat, he went to a nearby drugstore and got medication to give her by shots. We finally arrived at the hospital around midnight. When he and pastor Edwards saw that Susan was in good hands, they turned around and drove back to Lubbock that same night. This was just one example of the countless acts of kindness and concern that have strengthened us through the years.

CECIL. This was really a critical time for us. Susan had a collapsed lung and stayed in Houston again for nearly a month. After we arrived and got her settled in, Lanny and I went back to Lubbock where Lanny stayed with Charlene's parents until Charlene and Susan came home. For a time there, it seemed that we went from crisis to crisis during those first months, but looking back, they really weren't that close.

7

Victories Large and Small

When Cecil designed and built Baby, it opened up a whole area of freedom for the entire family. No longer tied to the cumbersome Emerson tank, they were able to travel. Their first trips, as you might imagine, were to San Angelo to see grandparents, Charlie and Ida Andrews, Charlene's parents, and to Comyn, Texas, to see Paul and Annie Ray, Cecil's parents. Later, after they gained confidence, they explored many avenues of travel adventure with Susan, the most enthusiastic traveler of all.

LANNY. I remember the summertime visits to our grandparents' homes. Texas is very hot in summer, and in those days most older homes had only one room that was air-conditioned. Susan and I were growing up in a house that was fully air-conditioned, so we tended to spend our time in that one cool room. When the grown-ups were busy with chores and catching up on family news, Susan and I would plant ourselves in front of the air conditioner and talk, tell stories, and laugh. We talked about schoolwork, who we liked and who we didn't, our friends, and things we hoped to do when we grew up.

Those summer days were free from the distractions of school and homework. There was little to claim our attention or interrupt us. Those were the good times, times when we got to be close and to really know each other. Today, they would call that brother-sister bonding, but all we knew was that we enjoyed being together.

Susan's plight had continued to capture the attention of the media, and a number of newspapers covered her progress regularly. Their accounts still bring to life those long and scary days when polio held America in the grip of fear.

Excerpts from the Lubbock-Avalanche Journal, *which were picked up by other Texas papers, reflect the interest Susan's illness continued to arouse:*

Visits to grandparents and other vacations are now possible for little Susan Ray, thanks to a new type of portable tank designed by her father and built in Lubbock. Travel, one of the greatest problems for iron lung patients, is now simply a matter of putting Susan in her iron lung and into the family station wagon and connecting the iron lung motor to the station wagon battery.

The new iron lung weighs about 135 pounds and can be carried, with Susan in it, by two men. The usual iron lung, in which she spent most of her time since stricken with polio in February of 1952, weighs about 900 pounds and requires 8–10 men to transport.

The Rev. Mr. Ray also designed and helped construct a rocking chair and motor light enough to be moved while Susan is rocking. The rocking chair, which is a breathing aid, was developed from the idea of the rocking bed which is used extensively for polio patients. Photographs of both were made at the Respiratory Center in Houston and are to be sent to equipment personnel at the National Foundation for Infantile Paralysis.

Susan had shown some improvement in both muscular ability and breathing in May when her most recent examination was made. She formerly was completely paralyzed but now has some slight use of her right hand and is beginning to practice writing. Gauze and a liquid which hardens are used so the pencil will stay in her hand. She will be six on July 14 and will begin first grade this fall, under the instruction of a private teacher.

As time passed, the public's interest in Susan continued. At least two Texas newspapers ran the following account of her sixth birthday party:

Luckiest Unlucky Girl—POLIO OR NOT, YOUNG LUBBOCK VICTIM ENJOYS BIRTHDAY PARTY

Susan Ray was six Tuesday—and she almost blew out all the candles on her cake without any help. . . .

The tiny polio victim has lived in an iron lung since February of 1952 when she was stricken with the disease, but she wasn't letting it distract her from her birthday.

Her cake, a large square with purple icing and "Happy Birthday, Susan" written on it, was brought in by her mother.

"Now, I'll blow out the candles," Susan said, "if it doesn't burn me up. That would be a mess now, wouldn't it?" she laughed.

She blew out two candles as fast as the respirator which controls her breathing would allow, then she paused. There was another special guest at Susan's party; ten-year-old Leon Elkins, an iron lung patient like Susan, was at the party in his portable respirator.

"Let Leon try one," Susan said. Leon blew out two and then the cake was handed back to Susan. She blew out candle number five but the last candle almost threw her.

Cecil's next project was to build a second, smaller tank respirator. This one hinged from the back and opened up, Susan said, "like an alligator." It had legs that could fold up for travel or hauling in the enclosed equipment trailer the Rays obtained. This respirator became the one most used for trips as Baby became Susan's every night tank. Cecil also built the first of several bath chairs which were simply aluminum stretchers with vinyl straps which could be set on a metal frame on the bath tub.

Plans for each of Cecil Ray's designs were offered to and featured in the **Toomey Gazette,** *a publication for polio victims and their caregivers. These plans were for use by anyone needing an item and were offered at no charge. Had he chosen to market the designs for the various types of equipment he designed through the years, no doubt Cecil would be a wealthy man today.*

CECIL. With that first trip when we returned to Houston in 1953, we had established the fact that we could travel safely and manage proper care for Susan in the car for an extended time. We had visited both sets of grandparents and now were ready for a bigger challenge. We felt it was important to offer as normal a life as possible to the children, and, frankly, Charlene and I needed some variety in our own lives.

Our first really daring trip was to Miami, Florida, in 1955 to attend the Baptist World Alliance. We had a brand new station wagon—a gift from friends and church members—which was air-conditioned and very roomy and comfortable. Although we felt that the traveling itself would pose no problems, what we had not yet done was to stay overnight in motels and eat our meals in restaurants. Nevertheless, we decided to give it a try. We invited my sister, Mary Ruth, to go with us. She had helped with Susan during those first weeks in the Lubbock hospital and was very good with her. This would be a three-week trip so we faced a number of new challenges and knew we could use her help.

During the course of a day's travel, we would stop at a roadside park and change her to her special chair in which she used her small chest shell respirator which could operate on a battery. Of course, this procedure caused a good bit of curiosity, no matter whether we stopped for the changeover, or for gas, or for meals.

When we finally arrived in Miami, Susan (with her battery-powered chest shell) was able to attend a few sessions, one in the Orange Bowl stadium. By now, we were accustomed to Susan and her Baby attracting a good bit of attention and having to make frequent explanations all along the way as people asked, "What on earth is THAT thing?"

While living in Lubbock, we also made a trip to Ruidoso, New Mexico. The cabin we stayed in belonged to the Henry Hecks, our associational WMU director and her husband, who offered us the use of it for a short vacation.

The doctors in Houston never commented much about our decision to travel with Susan, or our bent for developing ways to do things, until some time had passed. On a later checkup visit, they indicated that they had not been sure of the wisdom of our taking trips, but after several years of observing, had decided that we made the right decision, one that was good for Susan as well as for the entire family.

Although it meant disregarding most of what was known at that time about caring for respiratory polio patients, the Rays were determined to give their children a full life. Lanny was already showing evidence of a high IQ, and Susan, in spite of her limitations, was an intelligent and lively little girl who needed an outlet for her boundless curiosity and enthusiasm. The Rays set about to provide as rich and varied a life experience for the children as possible.

Prior to making these fun trips, Cecil had labored to make Susan a lightweight chair that could be used for sightseeing. In an effort to keep it light, it was designed with only three wheels, but was not too successful. In fact, it was not kept long, but long enough for four-year-old Lanny to tip it over and dump Susan on the sidewalk, giving her a black eye.

LANNY. I vaguely remember that chair with three wheels. I don't remember tipping Susan over, but I do remember her black eye and knowing that somehow I had something to do with it. I also remember the day I stepped on a clamp from that chair and cut my foot pretty badly. I still have that scar.

A sharper memory I have is of Susan's rocking chair that would swing up and down to help her breathing. I remember I would go outside to play and if a playmate wouldn't do what I wanted or something wouldn't go my way, I would come in, scuttle under the chair, and let it conk me on the head. Of course, my mother wasn't too pleased with this reaction to my frustration, but I didn't let it hit me so hard that it really hurt.

8
Preparing to Serve

CHARLENE. Time came for school to start. Susan would be a first grader and, as far as I could determine, she was as ready as any six year old. We lived just across an alley from the school, but, even so, Susan could not attend.

We knew Susan had a bright, inquisitive mind and were both determined that she should have every opportunity to develop that mind. To our delight, we learned that Lubbock had a homebound teacher for children unable to attend regular school. That was our answer.

Susan's teacher was a jewel. She taught and nurtured Susan and at least six other children in almost as many grades. She gave them parties in her backyard and spent time and effort to help them experience something of what school was like for the other children. Her interest in and encouragement of Susan played a large part in helping Susan reach out to the world beyond her confinement. Miss Katie Belle Crump was Susan's dear teacher until the spring of her third grade.

LANNY. I remember when Susan's teacher came to our home in Lubbock. She taught Susan in the big room that was also my playroom. I can't remember much that went on except for the math lessons. I was fascinated with math. When Miss Crump would sit down with the workbook and go through the exercises with Susan, I would listen carefully. Susan was always about four grades ahead of me, and later, when I was in school, I would look through the same math books and think how easy they were. So, I got an early exposure to math because of Susan's schooling, and as it turned out, I made that my career.

CHARLENE. Susan had another advantage during those early years. Marilyn, a girl scout who lived nearby, took Susan as a "project." She came once a week to play with her, reading stories, coloring, dressing dolls, whatever Susan wanted to do. Marilyn sparked Susan's first interest in Spanish when she brought us her little *Libro Uno* (*Book One*) which she had used in school earlier. Susan and Marilyn then began learning to read in Spanish, a skill Susan would use again and again through the years in carrying out her call to missionary service. Now, looking back, we can see God's hand at work, teaching, guiding, and preparing Susan so she could carry out His plan for her life, and we stand amazed at His faithfulness.

This early introduction to Spanish was undoubtedly God's preparation for a later ministry to a Hispanic church Susan and Charlene helped to start in Grand Prairie. Looking back through Susan's life, we can see the pattern of events that would shape her interests and her convictions.

Young though she was, Susan had a good grasp of spiritual things. When tenderhearted Lanny began to question things he had learned about the crucifixion of Jesus, Susan was able to help him understand the deep Scriptural truths involved, and he has never forgotten the things she taught him.

LANNY. When I learned in Sunday School about how Jesus died on the cross, I couldn't believe people could be that cruel to each other. To me, it just could not have happened. Susan assured me that "yes, it did happen," and it was something important we should all learn about and take seriously. She explained to me not just what occurred, but the significance of it. Of course, I didn't understand it all until years later, but I remember her "elderly-sister tutoring" which made more of an impression on me than all the Sunday School teachers and sermons I ever heard.

When Susan contracted polio in February 1952, scientists around the world had already been hard at work for over fourteen years in a concentrated effort to produce a safe and effective vaccine. Their efforts were controversial since little was known at that time about the nature of viruses, and no one knew if giving a vaccine of dead polio virus to a well child would cause the disease to develop. In America Dr. Jonas Salk and his assistants were working eighteen to twenty hours a day on the project.

By March 1954, plans were under way to test the Salk vaccine on several thousand school children. Because so little was known of its effects, the country was divided on whether or not such a vaccine should even be tested. Walter Winchell, a prominent newspaper and radio columnist, added greatly to the confusion with weekly comments. One

Sunday night he closed the first half of his broadcast saying, "In a few minutes I will report on a new polio vaccine announced as a polio cure. It may be a killer!" Then during the second half of his program, he continued, "Attention all doctors and every family in the United States. The United States Public Health Service," he said, "has found that seven out of ten batches of the Salk vaccine contained live virus. The polio foundation is trying to kill this story, but the U.S Public Health Service will confirm this in about ten days. Why wait ten days?"

He could have sabotaged the entire polio vaccination program but, thankfully, Winchell's report was in error. The three-part Salk vaccine, first given to 440,000 children in a controlled test, and then offered free of charge to children all across America, proved to halt the disease in its tracks. The March of Dimes raised over $50,000,000 in January 1955 to cover the costs of the massive inoculation program. Americans had rallied together and beat the terror, but tens of thousands of her best citizens were to pay the price of its bondage throughout their lives.

In 1956, the Rays moved to San Antonio where Cecil became superintendent of missions for the San Antonio Baptist Association. It was his responsibility to coordinate mission activities for the seventy churches in the association. He developed and launched an intensive study to learn the potential for future Baptist work in the area. This survey became a model used widely by other Baptist associations, both in Texas and across the nation.

CHARLENE. When we moved to San Antonio, I immediately called the San Antonio Board of Education to see if a homebound teacher were available. They informed me they already had their hands full—and an empty bank account—trying to educate all of San Antonio's diverse population. Yet, I was determined that Susan would receive as good an education as any child is given. The answer was clear. I would have to teach Susan myself.

My earlier experience teaching with Cecil in that tiny two-teacher school the second year of our marriage made me confident that I could fill the bill, so I went to the school where Lanny would begin first grade in the fall. The teachers were quite understanding and helpful, and assured me they would be of any help I might need.

I got the books I needed, including a Spanish primer. San Antonio required that Spanish be taught along with English in the elementary schools. We had chosen to use the same curriculum, so Susan would be studying the same subjects and books as her friends. Since we were already two years behind in curriculum Spanish, Susan and I completed three Spanish textbooks in that same year. It wasn't easy, but again, we can now look back and see God's hand at work, preparing her for the future.

Susan's schooling led us into a variety of experiences. For instance, when Susan reached her junior high years, our next-door neighbor, who was a college biology teacher, taught Susan science while I looked after her very active three year old. I learned that seeing to Susan's education entailed many other tasks besides teaching.

Despite Susan's inability to romp and play with other children, she had a happy childhood. She had numerous playmates who came to spend time with her and was actively involved in the children's programs in her family's church. Her favorite activity was to study about Baptist missionaries and their work around the world in what was then the "Sunbeams," and later in Girl's Auxiliary (GA, now known as Girls in Action). Through these programs of study, she learned about other countries, their foods and customs, and their great need to know Christ. She learned to pray for these people and for the missionaries who brought them the Gospel. Without doubt, the influence of these activities can be credited for her intense interest in missions throughout her life.

Susan attended worship services regularly and spent her early years seated at the end of a pew, rocking in her special chair while her pastor preached. She was not shy or self-conscious about how others might perceive her in church or anywhere; it was simply the way things were for her.

CECIL. That rocking chair had been my first attempt at welding aluminum, which is really quite tricky. It was a combination rocking chair and outdoor chair. It had large wheels and sturdy brakes like those on a wheelchair. The bed part of the chair was fixed to rock, which helped Susan in breathing and served to stimulate her circulation. Susan used this one as her "going to church" chair during the time we were in San Antonio. Her rocking was soon accepted by the church folk and only newcomers seemed to notice this "odd happening."

I learned to weld aluminum with a torch in order to build Susan's chairs lighter in weight and more compact. The process can be quite difficult and at first the man who showed me how was very reluctant, but he finally agreed to tell me what to watch out for in the welding process. When he had shown me, I went home to give it a try and had beginner's luck. Thus, I built this first lightweight chair which rolled uphill to church quite easily on bicycle wheels and rocked during services.

We used this as a travel chair during most of our five years in San Antonio. One day we encountered a minor crisis. We wanted to have lunch at Luby's Cafeteria but found we could not get Susan's chair with its big wheels through the door. This challenged me to design a smaller-base for her chair which would allow us entry into more places. We ended up with a multiple-use chair for travel, church, and shopping. Once again, "necessity was the mother of invention." Needless to say, we have enjoyed many luncheons and dinners at Luby's since that time.

As happened quite often, a family from Austin learned of Cecil's equipment building skills and asked for his help. They had a daughter a little younger than Susan who needed a chair designed to fit her size and special needs. The father made several trips from Austin, always chuckling at Cecil's "professional" directions. "First you cut a piece this size and then you make another just like it!" These instructions did make perfect sense, however. After all, both sides of a chair are identical. It was the development of this chair that later led to the San Antonio TV news feature and the follow-up newspaper coverage that resulted in Cecil being named "Father of the Year."

LANNY. It was while we lived in San Antonio that I became old enough to realize that my sister was different from other kids and that it wasn't normal to always be confined to a wheelchair. It began to dawn on me that our household wasn't like everybody else's either. In fact, no one else we knew had the equipment and gadgets we took for granted every day. Then I started to notice how other people looked at Susan, some with

Susan entertained "Amos" and "Kingfish" from radio's famous Amos and Andy show during their visit to San Antonio to appear in a fund-raiser for the March of Dimes.

puzzlement, others with curiosity or just plain "nosiness." I began to feel awkward and resentful of them; I wanted to tell them to mind their own business. Susan didn't seem to even notice them though.

So while I felt badly for her, I was always surprised to see how well she handled it. Both as a child and as an adult, she dealt with her condition with a maturity and style that have always amazed me. She would assure people that they need not be alarmed or feel sorry for her. She explained her condition and reminded them to be sure they had gotten all their immunizations. "That way you can make sure you will never get polio," she told them. She used their questions as an opportunity to help people understand and improve their lives. Even though young, Susan had already caught a glimpse of this as an opportunity to minister.

CHARLENE. Two memories that are precious to both Cecil and me are the times when Susan and Lanny professed their faith in Christ. They each took this step while we were attending Dellview Baptist Church in San Antonio; however, they did not make this decision at the same time. They were each about ten or eleven, the standard "junior" age when most Baptist youngsters think about making this decision.

Cecil and our pastor, Jake Setzer, baptized Susan together. Cecil spoke the words and together they lowered her completely under water, as is the Baptist way. One of Susan's small tanks was standing nearby just in case, but it was not needed. Her ability to "frog-breathe" carried her through. Cecil also baptized Lanny upon his profession of faith a few years later. That, too, is one of our precious memories.

CECIL. The Christmas Susan was eleven, we faced a small dilemma. Lanny, who was eight, was to receive his first bicycle, and we wanted Susan to have a "bicycle," too. Even more, we wanted to surprise them both. I began to tinker with switches I knew Susan could operate with her limited abilities. Since she had to be able to effectively work the switch controls, these could not be a total surprise, but she had no idea what they would be used for.

The goal was to make the chair as compact as possible, with the ability to turn in a small area with as little damage to the house inside as possible. The back wheels were limited in size to keep it narrow, yet make it negotiable outdoors as well as in the house. The motion required for Susan to turn and go back and forward was so small that people would stop, watch, and then ask, "How is she doing that?" They could not see the minute movements that triggered the action.

Getting the chair from San Antonio to San Angelo for Christmas, along with Lanny's bike, was also quite a task. Since we always pulled an equipment trailer for Susan's big tank, our clothes, and other needs, we knew we had to arrange things differently this time. Susan was now able to travel with her chest shell except when she was sick, but we told her she had to ride in her "travel tank" in the car, thus making room for the two bicycles in the trailer.

LANNY. That motorized chair provided Susan with a tremendous step forward in her ability to interact with me and the other kids. I took these things for granted then, but now, looking back at how kids play and relate to one another, I realize it was a quantum leap for her. One of the games we liked best was our version of football. I would kick off to her by placing the ball in her lap. Then she would try to run in her chair, and I would crawl to make the speeds more equal. We had a great time playing that. Also, when outside with other kids, we would ride our bikes, and she would drive her chair around with us. She felt pretty much on an equal par with us then, and I believe this was very important to her in growing up. It sure made things more fun for everybody.

When we visited my mother's parents in San Angelo, we would race around an open space on their land in what we called our "Indy 500." I liked that as much as Susan did. I got to run fast and she enjoyed keeping up with me. These are among my best childhood memories of life with Susan.

Having and being able to operate her bicycle was the nearest thing for Susan to being as active as the other children, and doubtless played a big part in her happy childhood memories. While many quadriplegics had motorized chairs to help in work and everyday chores, Susan saw her chair as an important toy. On one occasion, she backed Lanny into a corner so that he had to call for help. She always laughingly remembered that as the one time she got even with her brother.

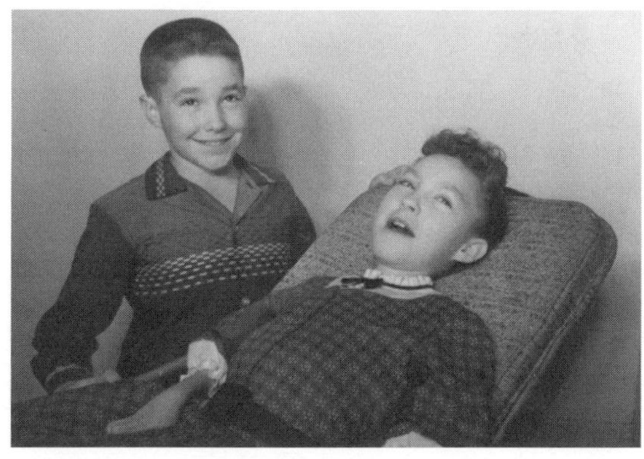

Susan and Lanny. Up to their pranks?

CHARLENE. One day when Cecil came home, Susan met him, all excited and eager to tell him about her day.

"Daddy, I got a spanking today for running away," she told him excitedly. She had been playing in the yard and on the sidewalk with friends, and, even though she could maneuver her bike well on sidewalks, I had told her not to go beyond the limit of our yard. When the other children ran to the end of our long block, Susan followed. I got quite a scare when I came out to check on her and Lanny. When I got them back home, I gave her a spanking of sorts to remind her to stay close by.

CECIL. In more recent years, with the development of more efficient and smaller positive pressure units, Susan could have had a motor chair with a breathing unit that operated off batteries, thus giving her even more mobility. However, while she would have enjoyed this extra freedom, she saw being able to write, type, paint, and cross-stitch as more important than having a motor chair.

The San Antonio years (1956–1961) were fruitful for the Ray family. In 1960, Cecil was named "Texas Baptist Father of the Year." This was due to the intensive and creative efforts he had made to assist Susan in living as full a life as possible. Excerpts from the statewide coverage tell the full story:

Working on weekends, the 38 year old has built an ingenious chair, three iron lungs, chest respirators, a mechanical desk, and assorted chairs and bathing equipment.

With the slight movement she can muster, Susan can now write and is learning to paint, using her special desk. Tilting her head from side to side, she touches more delicate switches which move the desk across the small area in which her tiny fingers can move.

A committee selected Ray as Father of the Year because of his "significant applications of Christian faith in helping his daughter overcome severe handicaps." The award is sponsored each year by the Baptist Standard and the Baptist General Convention of Texas on behalf of the denomination's 1.5 million members.

9

The Calling Made Clear

CECIL. During our years in San Antonio and later in Grand Prairie, we made numerous summer trips to Glorieta Baptist Conference Center near Santa Fe, New Mexico. In early years, while living in San Antonio, we would rent the Old Ranch House on the conference grounds and, together with the Mojica family, would attend Home Mission Week. For both Lanny and Susan, this trip was the highlight of the year. In 1958, when Susan was eleven, Glorieta provided Susan with what was to be the central thrust of her life.

One morning, at the conclusion of a worship service for children and youth, Susan felt God's call to serve Him through missions. We have no idea how she proposed to be able to do this and even less idea what those in charge of the program must have felt as they saw this young quadriplegic being pushed down to the front to give her life to missions, but we do know that Susan had her friend, Becky Mojica, to push her wheelchair down the aisle so she could respond to a call from God.

Charlene and I rejoiced with Susan, of course, although at that time none of us could understand what this meant or how God would enable Susan to fulfill such a commitment. However, we knew that God knew and that Susan was willing. It may all sound too simple, but we believed that was all that mattered. Somehow, someway, God would honor her decision. The only questions were when and how. Our task was not to question, or to even understand it all, but to help enable her in every way possible.

Now, many years later, we can see the clear direction of our Heavenly Father for Susan—and the ways in which Susan responded to His call. Each year, until her final illness, Susan discovered new and different ways in which God could use her as a voice for Christian missions, as well as for Christian concerns about the environment and the wrongs in society today. Commissioned only by God, Susan found ways to serve, and others saw her commitment and deemed her a missionary indeed.

Susan had no knowledge at that time of Charlene's earlier commitment to God to use her life in caring for her daughter. And, like Susan, neither Cecil nor Charlene could foresee the many ways God would open opportunities far and wide for Susan to champion and become personally involved in missions. Charlene passed on to Susan her love of reading and learning and her skill in writing. Although confined for most of her life, Susan became broadly educated and learned to write in both English and Spanish as outlets for her calling. Her contributions eventually covered broad areas of Christian ethics, churchmanship, and stewardship, as well as missions.

CHARLENE. When Susan wasn't studying, she spent lots of time being Lanny's "watch me" buddy and advice giver as he built all sorts of mazes and secret hideouts of chairs, sofa pillows, boxes, and such in our big den. They did all kinds of things together and were as close as any brother and sister can be. They learned to play checkers, but, of course, Lanny had to move Susan's, so she sometimes accused him of moving where she didn't intend.

One year the local Ford Motor Company wanted to donate a small battery-driven model of their new Ford convertible to the March of Dimes. It was made of fiberglass and had gotten damaged. Since Cecil had mastered the art of working with fiberglass, they asked him to repair the little car. In exchange, Lanny got the privilege of driving the car for a few weeks. Since it was winter, he could only ride it in our double garage. We still have pictures of Susan propped up beside him as they rode round and round, giggling with glee.

LANNY. In spite of her handicaps and her more serious side, Susan was full of mischievous fun. Mother frequently had woman's missionary meetings at our house, and Susan was my baby-sitter except when the other ladies brought their kids to stay with us in Susan's big room. Then we both became sitters. There was one boy in particular that we both dreaded coming because he was just a little terror. I still remember, after all these years, how we reacted when we heard he was coming. "Trouble tonight!" we would say and roll our eyes in unison. When there were no other children with us during those meetings, Susan encouraged me to choose a quiet activity and entertain myself since she liked to listen to the program to learn more about mission needs and the lives of those who served as missionaries. These were subjects she never tired of.

We delighted to go shopping with Mother. We would slip away through the grocery or department store and find an open aisle which we would race down as fast as I could push Susan. The faster the better for Susan. She loved it, but I'm sure we were a trial to Mother. Another big part of growing up with Susan was playing table games. There she was equal with anybody. Checkers, Chinese checkers, chess, dominoes, Scrabble—she was a whiz at them all. Our game playing extended from the time I entered school through high school. By the time I started college, I had little time for games, but even recently when we would get together, out came the game boards again.

CHARLENE. During her school days in San Antonio, I discovered that Susan had a definite aptitude for writing. Cecil's associate, Mike Mojica, and his family lived across the street from us. They had two sons, Tommy and Mickey, who were Lanny's best friends, and a daughter, Becky, who was one of Susan's best friends. Cheryl, who lived just down the street, was her other best friend.

One summer, some time after Susan had made her commitment to missions, we learned there would be a conference for writers at Glorieta. We decided it would be good for Susan to be exposed to the possibilities of writing as an outlet for her mission concerns. We knew it would help us, too, since Cecil's work involved some writing of stewardship materials.

During the youth meetings that week, Susan felt a second call from God. This call to serve with Spanish-speaking people was in addition to her earlier, more general call to serve in Christian missions. Her two callings met at that conference that summer, but they remained to be carried out after we moved to Grand Prairie. Again, we could not look ahead and know exactly how God would use her, but Susan remained convinced of her calling. She never doubted that God had chosen her to serve Him with her life.

LANNY. Our trips to Glorieta were some of our best times. The climate at Glorieta was cool and dry, just right to enjoy in summer. Even though the terrain was pretty rugged, there were a few trails we could take Susan on. One trail we explored with her took us to a point where we could get a breathtaking view of the valley below. We never tired of pushing Susan in her chair to see the play of changing light and shadows over the valley. Most of the time though, she and Becky stayed inside, doing whatever it is that teenage girls do. I've never quite figured that out, even though I have a teenager of my own now.

Soon after Susan experienced her second call, Cecil developed a miniature remote keyboard for a typewriter that was given to Susan by

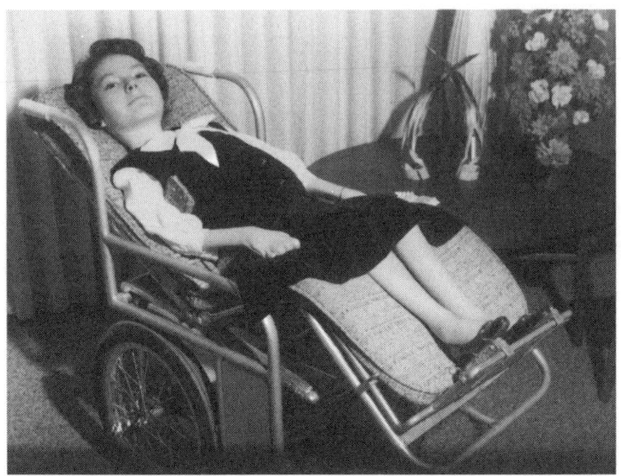

*Teenage Susan dressed and ready
for a church banquet.*

*the pastors of the San Antonio Baptist Association. Having this type-
writer opened a whole new world of involvement for Susan, first
assisting her in her schoolwork and ultimately becoming her "voice" as
she determined to express her convictions and concerns to the world at
large, even though rarely could she express them in person.*

*The typewriter was central to Susan's special callings. Many handi-
capped individuals have turned to the typewriter as a means of
communicating with the world. Some have learned to type with a stylus
held and controlled by their mouth, others with the stylus held firmly in
place by a band around the forehead, and still others with it held by their
toes. In every case, the trick is to determine what each individual's best
remaining skill might be and link to this. For Susan, it was her right hand,
with her arm suspended in a sling that supported her hand, yet allowed
for some up and down movement. While Susan could not make these
movements without the arm bars and a sling, she could, with this help,
control her hand movement to the selected keys and type. She also used a
similar application to paint, draw, embroider, and even do some writing.*

CECIL. It was about 1958 when we came to the conclusion that Susan
needed a typewriter—if we could figure out a way for her to use one. Of
course, the electric typewriter was the in thing then; computers were not
yet on the market. I called the man who was in charge of San Antonio's
IBM maintenance and repair. My first question was, "How does an electric typewriter work?" You could almost feel from the silence that the
man was thinking, "What kind of nut is this?" However, he was cour-
teous and after learning the why of my question, engaged his team of
regular servicemen in brainstorming with me.

It was decided that I should build a small remote keyboard to fit Susan's range of motion. Instead of keys, her keyboard would be composed of holes. With a stylus, she would make electrical contact with an attachment under the typewriter to pull down the keys and type. The men at IBM sold us a good used typewriter and then rigged and installed the attachment for Susan to use. Interested people in San Antonio paid for the typewriter and other needed parts.

Susan's range of motion was about one and one-half inches high and three and one-fourth inches wide, so the keyboard had to be very small. We rearranged the letters so the most used were the easiest to reach. Susan quickly learned to type and soon was able to do her schoolwork and some of her first efforts at letters and stories.

An article concerning Susan and the equipment that enabled her appeared about that time in **The Window,** *which was then the national magazine for Baptist Young Women. It quotes Charlene as she explains something of Cecil's efforts to provide Susan with the tools she needed to develop to her fullest potential:*

> We never want people to think that my husband has provided Susan's equipment alone. Without the help of many friends who have given liberally of money, materials, labor, and prayer, we would still be using hospital equipment loaned by the National Foundation for Infantile Paralysis and living a limited life. But these gifts, coupled with faith, determination, and the creative ability of my husband, make possible a house full of gadgets and a rich life, full of fun and adventure.

CECIL. The scope and depth of interest and concern for Susan through the years have continued to amaze us. For example, from the beginning of her bout with polio, the people of Lubbock and even across the state kept tabs on her progress. Nearly every time she became ill, the newspapers wanted daily reports on her, and many people we knew only slightly or not at all wanted to be a part in helping us. Looking back, we can clearly see how God used the kindness of thoughtful people to help meet our special needs.

One example: when I returned to Lubbock from Houston the first time after leaving Susan and Charlene at the center there, Mack Mead, of Mead's Bakery, handed me an envelope with his air-travel card enclosed and a note insisting I use his card to pay for all my trips back and forth to see Susan. His brother, Bill Mead, had already loaned us his vacation house in New Mexico for a vacation one summer before Susan had polio.

And the Meads were not even members of our church. Another unexpected blessing was that First Baptist in Lubbock had continued to pay Mrs. Herod's salary and gave her time off to help Charlene with Susan during her first two weeks in the Lubbock hospital.

In the years after, when Susan was back at home, this interest in her never seemed to wane. Everywhere we have lived, people have been caring and concerned, but especially so in Lubbock. The preacher in me cannot help but compare this to the caring exhibited by the early Christian church. It is hard to explain how much this support has meant to all of us, but we believe it has been prompted by the Father's love and are thankful to Him and to each of these who has shared His love with us.

CHARLENE. Many think that paralyzed people have little or no feeling in those areas of the body that cannot move, but that usually isn't true. Susan seldom experienced pain, but we were often summoned, even during the night, to scratch her nose, or arm, or leg. Usually, her calls for assistance were minor, but on one occasion, we once again faced a crisis. Susan had been experiencing some pain and swelling in her abdomen which did not respond to anything we tried. At first, we feared locked bowels, but when she did not respond to the doctor's treatment, he suggested we contact the hospital in Houston. We called and they said, "Come immediately!" Susan needed immediate surgery.

When we arrived in late afternoon, they were ready for us. The operation lasted for hours as we alternately assured one another that things would be fine, and then paced the halls in a vain effort to hurry time. When the doctors came to report that all went well, they told us they had removed an ovarian cyst the size of a grapefruit. How thankful we were that, bad as it was, it was something that could be taken care of. During recovery, Susan was visited by processions of medical students wanting to meet the tiny girl who had such a large cyst and who was even in an iron lung.

LANNY. I was in the fifth grade when we made that emergency trip to Houston. I knew Susan had been ill but was surprised when someone came into my room at school and told me that Susan needed emergency surgery. I was excited about getting out of school to head for Houston, but I was also scared for Susan.

When I got home, we piled into the car for a three-to-four hour trip. Of course, I had no idea what an ovarian cyst was nor how dangerous giving anesthesia to a person like Susan could be in those days. I do remember the nearly six-hour wait for surgery to be completed seemed like days and days. When it was all over and we knew she was safe, we spent the night with Houston friends. I still remember the outpouring of concern that came from friends, church members, and folk from all over Texas, some of whom we didn't even know!

Despite her limitations, Susan was always active in all areas of her church's programs, especially those that relate to missions. She was crowned GA Queen in a church-wide recognition service along with other girls who had completed the "Forward Steps" set forth by the Girl's Auxiliary organization. These steps required a candidate for Queen to memorize extensive Scripture passages, write an essay detailing her conversion experience, and participate in mission outreach activities. Needless to say, this award entailed a great deal of effort, but Susan completed each one exactly as set forth. Her interest in missions continued to grow, and, as she matured, she became even more active in YWA's, the young woman's mission organization. Susan loved socials and other special occasions at church, often helping to plan them. Among her favorites was a "tacky party" given while she was a part of YWA's (now Acteens), where she dressed up as a very creditable tramp. During her Raleigh years, she served as bridesmaid in a friend's wedding. Charlene had to split open a large white, broad-brimmed hat so Susan

Susan at age sixteen attending a Girls in Action Hobo Party in Grand Prairie, Texas.

could wear it while lying in her chair, but as usual, the two of them found a way to get around any snag they encountered.

LANNY. Susan and I were siblings, but I did not know what that meant as a little boy; all I knew was that Susan was my older sister and that she was my super good friend. When everyone else was busy doing things that have to be done in a family, Susan was always there for me—to talk to me and listen to me, to share the wisdom of her advanced years, to watch me play and appreciate how well I built forts of stacked blocks or rode my trike. She was there when I wanted to play games with someone and she taught me several that I might not have thought of—even though we had to adjust some processes so that I could move or play for both of us. She was my friend who let me play with her but who also let me play alone when that suited me. She gave me room to be me but was very much a part of my life.

While Susan was busily involved in church activities where she was beginning to take leadership roles, I became interested in building and launching rockets. I was a first grader when Sputnik was launched by the Russians, and I remember searching the sky at night to see if I could get a glimpse of that little ball flying around the earth so fast and so high. I was fascinated to hear of Alan Shepherd and his suborbital flight and of John Glenn and others as they added to American prestige through their experiences in space. I could hardly wait until I was grown and could be involved in the space program.

Because of my excitement about the space program, dime-store toys that looked like rocket ships that you flew in your hand while you said "vroom," didn't satisfy me for long. I wanted to build something that could actually be launched just like they did at Cape Canaveral. Mine would be of more limited size, of course, but they had to fly and fly high, —much higher than would have been good for my health or our neighborly relations if I fired them off from my yard. I needed a good deal of space since my guidance systems were not quite as sophisticated as those of NASA. Since I was too young to drive but had to get my rockets to some wide-open spaces, I recruited Susan to cheer and "ooh" and "aah," and Mother to do all the above and also to drive. Whenever I built new rockets, we would drive out to a friend's cow pasture in the country, and I would blast off with wide-eyed cows watching from the other side of the fence.

One day, we loaded up a three- or four-pound rocket I had built and headed for the launch site. I could hardly wait to blast off this new multi-engine model. When we arrived, we got Susan out of the car and placed her chair nearby. As I was getting everything ready, I was giddy with excitement over what I knew would be a triumphal flight. Mother and Susan would love this one; it was going to be great!

I stationed myself about fifty yards away, both to get a good view and to better receive radio signals from a transmitter on board the rocket. When everything was ready, I signaled Mother to fire the engines and up it went. It took off perfectly and flew like an arrow, but, suddenly, something went wrong. One of the engines blew up! To my absolute horror, it topped out, veered over, and headed straight for Susan's chair. My heart, already pounding from the excitement of the launch, was now in my throat; I could do nothing but watch in horror as the burning wreckage of my former missile headed straight for Susan.

I was terrified and would have cried if it would have done any good. The rocket spiraled madly, but though it was plummeting toward earth, it seemed to take forever. Then just as I thought I would burst with fear, it spiraled again and crashed a few feet from Susan. I was so relieved that it was a few moments before I even thought about what was left of my rocket. Mother and Susan seemed to have lost their enthusiasm for any more launches that day, too. We were just glad to get back home, shaken but thankfully unbloodied. I had an idea it would take a little bit of persuasion to get Mother and my sister out on a rocket launch with me anytime soon.

In 1961, Cecil accepted a position as head of the Cooperative Program and Church Finance Department, Stewardship Division, Baptist General Convention of Texas. The Ray family moved to Grand Prairie, a small town some twenty-two minutes from the Baptist Building in Dallas. Susan was fourteen at the time and studying on a high-school level, taking the same subjects and using the same textbooks as girls her age in public school.

LANNY. We moved to Grand Prairie the summer between my fifth and sixth grades. My first summer there was very lonely. I had left my friends behind and didn't know a soul. We had nice neighbors, and I made new friends when school started, but Susan was clearly my best friend that summer. We spent most of every day together, talking, playing games and watching far too much of the Three Stooges on television.

CHARLENE. During the early 1960s, when Susan was in her early teens, she began to voice some of her social concerns. She and Lanny were alike in their thinking, and both became ardent supporters of integration. Lanny was concerned that our church had only white members so he went to his school superintendent, who was a deacon, and learned that sometime before our coming, the church had voted not to accept black members. Lanny decided it was time to make his views known. He and some of his friends went around to the various Sunday School departments trying to persuade them to change the vote. Susan would have gone too, but wasn't able, so she gave Lanny and his friends lots of encouragement. She would have loved to be able to go and express her strong convictions for herself, but knew she could rely on Lanny to make her views known The vote was never changed, but I don't think there were any black persons who even wanted to come to that church anyway.

LANNY. Since Susan was older than I, we were never in the same classes at church until after I graduated from high school. The Dallas area as a whole was extremely conservative in those days, and, coupled with that, I was in a conservative Baptist church. I found myself in an arena where my ideas on Vietnam, race relations, and economics were not met with open arms. In fact, I met with some hostility, but Susan was my sounding board and advocate, and supported my right to hold forth my carefully thought-out ideas.

We had lively discussions in Training Union on Sunday evenings about all that was going on in the world, and spent a good deal of time thinking and questioning and considering how best to react to different issues. There were a lot of closed minds and crazy ideas among us, but Susan always took the level-headed approach. She often acted as moderator between the conservative adults who led the discussions and the younger adults who saw things differently. Her calm way of heading off confrontation was helpful for everybody and encouraged us to consider all sides of the issues. Without a doubt, this sister of mine, although confined and scarcely able to move, was the least fettered of us all.

Of real concern to the Ray family after moving to Grand Prairie were the power shortages that accompanied the frequent and intense summer storms there. The power was prone to go off and on without warning, often staying off for quite some time. Unfortunately, Grand Prairie did not have the dual electrical systems that were available in Lubbock, but once again, the thoughtfulness of friends came through. One of the men from the church the Rays attended helped Cecil connect up an additional generator, making sure Charlene and Lanny understood how to operate it to provide dc voltage for Susan's breathing gear when Cecil was out of town. That unit underwent a severe test when Hurricane Carla came barreling through Texas with the eye maintaining itself all the way through to Dallas and passing right over Grand Prairie. This could have been a terrifying time for Susan and her family, but the auxiliary unit had already proven itself and so the Rays did not worry.

During these years, Susan broadened her concept of missions, writing letters and submitting articles to various publications, hoping to win an audience. She dealt with aspects of life that are not always seen as mission objectives but believed her faith was broad enough to cover every facet of life.

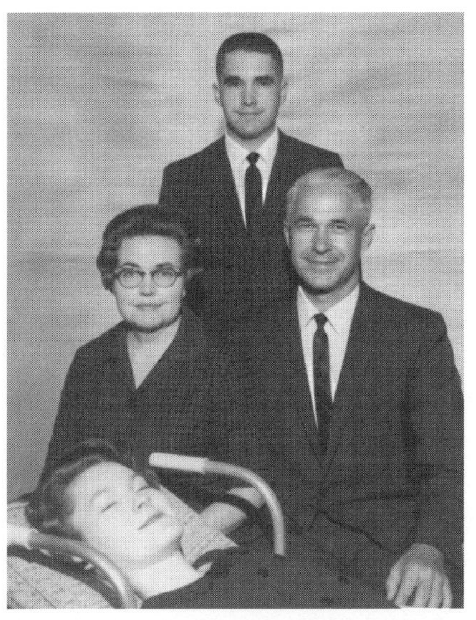

This family portrait was taken while the Rays were in Grand Prairie, Texas.

CHARLENE. Cecil was forty-four in 1968 when he was named director of the Stewardship Division of the State Missions Commission for Texas Baptists. His tasks included challenging individual Baptists and their churches to deepen their stewardship commitments. Soon after Cecil started work in the Stewardship Division, he found the need to produce a variety of materials for both education and promotion. I did his proofing and corrections for a time, but we soon turned most of it over to Susan. She quickly saw these tasks as part of the fulfilling of her calling and she was "off and running."

During those years, we turned out an extensive library of audio-visuals. Susan wrote a number of filmstrip narrations and a short motion picture script in addition to mountains of other materials, some of which were used by the Southern Baptist Stewardship Commission and distributed to other states. Susan finally became her dad's proofreader, rewriter, and coauthor. Nothing he wrote left the house without her final okay.

Cecil and I still worked together on some projects, however. We developed a special study entitled *Christian Family Money Management*, which was used extensively by Texas Baptists, as well as other state conventions, for a number of years. Cecil also wrote *Living the Responsible Life*, which was taught to furloughing missionaries and has been translated into Spanish, Korean, and several African languages. Another widely used publication, coauthored by Cecil and Susan, is *Cooperation—the Baptist Way to a Lost World*.

The Rays were a prolific team. Their collective work during those years helped challenge Baptists to review their giving commitment, which led to an increase in Texas Baptist Cooperative Program offerings from $10,188,000 to $22,200,000 in the fourteen years Cecil served in this position. The materials they developed were used successfully in other states as well.

CHARLENE. In 1967, Cecil made mission tours of Spain and Africa to report back firsthand to stateside Baptists on the progress their mission efforts were making there. While there, of course, he was asked to preach and was rewarded by seeing people from these other cultures come to know the Lord. Several of these contacts have bloomed into lifelong friendships. One was when Cecil met Douglas Waruta in Africa.

CECIL. Douglas was a young pastor in Nyeri, Kenya. He had studied at the Baptist Theological Seminary of East Africa in Tanzania but longed to study in the United States. A missionary arranged for Douglas to come to Hardin-Simmons University in Abilene, Texas, where a group of interested people undertook his sponsorship. We were part of that group.

Douglas visited with us as he could while in the States. He and Susan seemed to develop an especially close bond, sharing long, serious conversations, although we all felt very close to this fine young man so far away from home and family. When Douglas received his degree, he returned to Nairobi, Kenya, married, and became the father of two sons, James and Benjamin. Our friendship has continued to grow, even across the miles and the years, and the Waruta family still plays an ongoing role in the life of our family.

CHARLENE. When we first moved to Grand Prairie, we had made the same arrangements for Susan's schooling as we had in San Antonio. The high school principal was a member of our church. When Susan expressed a desire to visit a class, he made all the arrangements. She enjoyed the fellowship with the class members but was disappointed in the classes themselves. They were quite a bit behind us, and she quickly became bored since she had already covered that material.

When school was out that year, some of her friends asked Susan, "What happened after? . . . We didn't get to finish our history book before school closed." Susan was able to tell them the rest of the story, and I think it did her good to know she wasn't missing out on too much by having me as her teacher. I had made her read every page and work every problem in all her texts, so she was very familiar with what they had

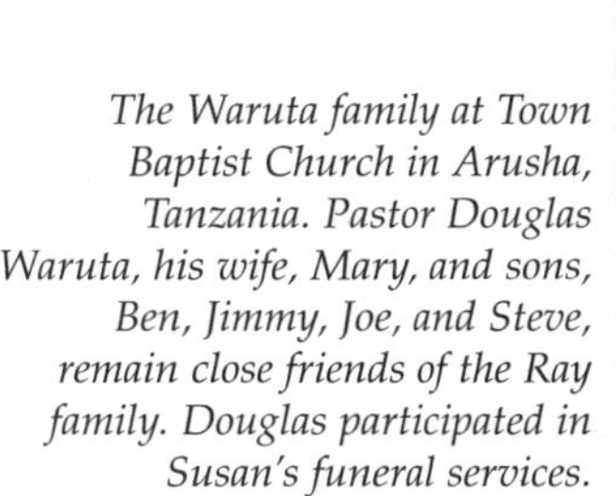

The Waruta family at Town Baptist Church in Arusha, Tanzania. Pastor Douglas Waruta, his wife, Mary, and sons, Ben, Jimmy, Joe, and Steve, remain close friends of the Ray family. Douglas participated in Susan's funeral services.

learned and more. When graduation came, Susan received her diploma just like the rest of them. After graduation, I bowed out as teacher and Susan began taking college correspondence courses. She did not choose the traditional college curriculum but studied and made good grades in her areas of special interest: English, Bible, journalism and Spanish.

LANNY. When Susan was in her mid-teens and I was old enough to know a little about this boy/girl thing, I remember a church social where Susan was hurting because all her friends had boyfriends and she didn't. It was not that she wasn't realistic about her limitations. She understood that was just not going to be a part of her life, but still it hurt. I didn't fully understand it at the time, but she definitely liked boys and had all those normal feelings of growing up. Not being able to enjoy these relation- ships was something she had to learn to live with, or in this case, to live without. She understood these things though and was always ready to help me think them through.

I was very shy as a teenager, especially around girls. I remember one church function where everyone was supposed to bring a date. I had an awful crush on one girl and asked her to go with me, but she had already accepted another boy's invitation, so she turned me down. I was devas- tated and thought my life was over. Again, Susan came to my rescue saying, "Don't worry. It's not that big of a deal. Just ask somebody else." Her advice was good, but I didn't take it. It was many years before I regained enough confidence to take a girl out.

Beginning in the mid-1960s, Cecil chaired a little-known committee composed of Texas laymen who were skilled in electronics. Their task was to explore the best ways for Baptist churches and mission outposts to take advantage of electronic technology, majoring in the use of the audio cassette. They pioneered the use of audio tapes for shut-ins and others unable to attend regular worship services. They developed a packaged cassette player with built-in amplifiers to be used in the African bush and other isolated mission outposts. Without doubt, Cecil's knack for things mechanical carried over into this Christian endeavor as well, and proved to be a real blessing in mission outreach as well as in meeting Susan's changing needs, for as she matured, the pattern of her breathing and her requirements for adequate air changed as well.

CECIL. Susan first began using positive pressure in 1961. Up until this time, she had used the chest shell which was operated by a negative pressure (suction) unit. The chest shell does for the limited part of the body which it covers what the big tanks do by causing a vacuum which pulls air into the lungs. Ten years of using negative pressure had enlarged Susan's rib cage considerably, and her doctors felt it essential that we substitute positive pressure to assist her in breathing.

Positive pressure units are very simple in concept. They act much like what one would have by attaching a hose at the blowing end of a vacuum cleaner, but with a rotating air release valve to cause air to be blown in only during the breath-intake cycle. Susan learned to accommodate this system and found it not only simpler, but more comfortable and effective. It also simplified her clothing since she no longer needed to wear the chest shell under her outfit. This one change made both breathing and getting dressed for the day much easier.

Susan used the Bantam positive pressure units from 1961 to 1992. During most of this time, the two units we kept on hand were provided by the March of Dimes. In more recent years, the March of Dimes transferred their equipment to Lifecare, a company established to handle and provide this kind of respiratory equipment. The March of Dimes, however, continued to provide these units for Susan until she became eligible for Medicare. After that, rental payments came from Medicare, our personal health insurance, and our personal funds.

LANNY. When I got into my college years, it suddenly dawned on me that if anything happened to Mom and Dad, I would be the one to care for Susan. It hit me like a ton of bricks as I realized this isn't at all like caring for a younger sibling. This would be a major deal! As a college kid, I was nowhere near prepared for such responsibility. Of course, we did have lots of relatives we could call on who would come in an instant until

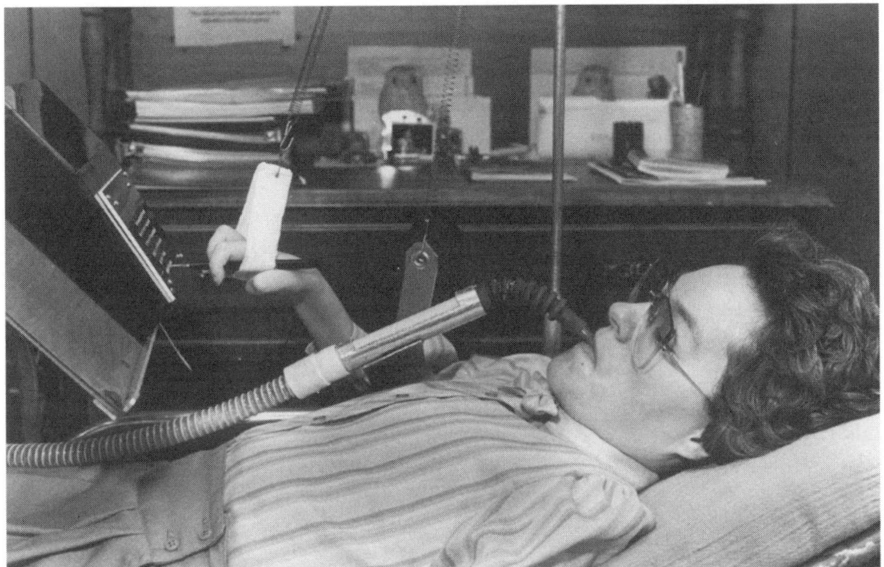

As technology improved, Susan's father was able to make her equipment even more efficient—
Courtesy Southern Baptist Historical Library and Archives.

we had things worked out, so I didn't worry for too long, but it was always something I kept in the back of my mind. Susan's care would entail a huge responsibility; however, the idea that she might go into an institution was unthinkable. I simply would not let that happen.

Every time I thought about the responsibility of caring for Susan by myself, I would remind myself that my Dad had lived with this responsibility since he was a young man and had made a full, productive life for himself and for us. Susan and I had just grown up taking for granted that her needs would be met, but I now realized it had not come easily for either of my parents.

Suddenly, the not-so-simple mechanics of her equipment, keeping it working, providing for back-ups in case something broke, all seemed overwhelming. Whenever I would think about all this and realize it was far too big a task for me to handle, my faith in the Lord took over and I said, "Okay, Lord, I believe You'll get us through this if it happens." Deep down, I knew that if such a dilemma came up, it would have worked out just fine because of Susan's temperament and her willingness to make the best of any situation. Her positive mental approach to every challenge made the physical problems easier to deal with.

10
Face-to-Face Ministry

CHARLENE. It was while we were in Grand Prairie that Susan was first able to carry out the commitment to Hispanic missions she had made at Glorieta earlier. A young lady in our church had a friend whose father brought groups of men up from Mexico to work in his construction business. In those days, there were no strict regulations concerning illegal immigrants. In fact, many of these men also worked for the city of Grand Prairie on the garbage trucks.

When we learned that Jettie Winston was planning to start a mission for these Spanish-speaking workers, Susan and I offered our services. First Baptist Church would sponsor the mission, and we would meet in a vacant house the church owned just across the parking lot. Jettie's husband would drive the church bus to pick up the men every Sunday morning. We knew we could get someone to preach in Spanish from the Language Missions Department in Dallas.

At first, we used the tiny living room of the house for worship services, which was enough room when only the men came. One morning, to our delight, some other people came, families and women with children. One young woman came with a baby and sat in the front row. When the baby became fretful, she put him down to crawl around, After that, the preacher had to watch his step carefully if he moved the least bit from his pulpit, which was a little lectern stand.

When the little house became too small to serve the growing congregation, we moved into an old building the church owned that was rat infested. A dog next door bit the organist one Sunday morning so the situation was somewhat less than ideal. Once we even came to church and found that vandals had shot holes in the front door, but we continued to grow. Once we got a full-time pastor, he insisted that we move over to the chapel of First Baptist until we could obtain a building of our own. We finally got a beautiful, little, red-brick church in the far corner of the First Baptist Church property, and we were delighted.

Susan had been teaching the children at Mision Bautista on Sunday nights from the very beginning. Now she had a nice place for her class. Together, she and I took charge of all the children and youth, nursery through high school, on Wednesday nights as well. The parents wanted their children taught in English, but in spite of their requests, we tried to teach them a few hymns in Spanish. Otherwise, they would have understood nothing of what was being said in the Spanish worship services. Susan also introduced them to sign language during Church Training on Sunday nights, and sometimes we saw them trying to communicate by sign language across the church during worship services.

After some years at Mision Bautista, two of our Hispanic friends, Dora Fuentes and Paul Martinez, declared we were not Anglos anymore. What a compliment! They could see how much we loved their children. In fact, the pastor christened me "Old Mother Hen." We never really learned to speak Spanish fluently, but we could read it and understood the sermons fairly well. Before we left for North Carolina, almost every one of the children we had worked with had made a profession of faith and been baptized. Since the pastor's wife was their Sunday School teacher, Susan and I would not dream of claiming the credit, but I like to think we helped.

Susan saw drama as an important tool in ministry. She and I wrote a number of Christmas pageants in Spanish for this church. Years later, Susan and I entered one of these Christmas dramas in a contest sponsored by the Spanish Publishing House in El Paso, Texas, and it won second place. For one of the many filmstrips Susan wrote for the Baptist General Convention of Texas, members of Mision Bautista posed as the Macedonian Christians.

In 1968, Cecil was awarded an honorary doctorate by Howard Payne College, his alma mater. Later, in 1978, while serving in North Carolina, he was given the Distinguished Alumni Award from Southwestern Baptist Theological Seminary.

In 1990, he was again honored by Howard Payne, now a university, at their Distinguished Alumni Banquet. After being introduced to the large audience, Cecil was given a plaque and wristwatch in acknowledgment of his outstanding service to Baptists. In no small way, these recognitions and awards also honored the strong, resourceful family members who have played so large a part in his endeavors. Rather than being deterred by the needs that Susan's care required, it seems these became a spur to encourage the entire family to become more involved with needs outside their own home.

CHARLENE. Upon graduating from high school, Lanny attended the University of Texas at Arlington, where he received a degree in aerospace

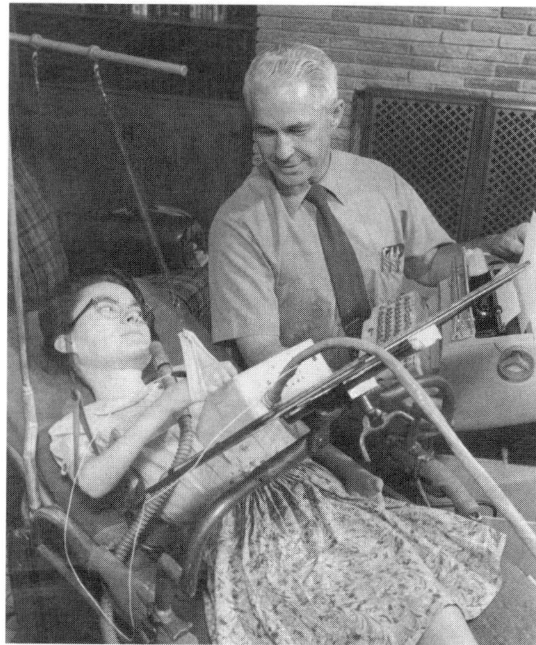

Susan's father designed her first typewriter when she was thirteen. Shown here at age twenty-seven, she demonstrated how she was able to produce the numerous materials she developed for Christian and environmental causes.

engineering. He was the first engineering student ever to have completed all courses there with a perfect grade-point average. After he entered graduate school at the University of Texas in Austin, he came home only some weekends until he met Mary Gomez.

Their meeting was almost accidental. Lanny's best friend, Paul, wanted to date Linda Gomez, who agreed, provided it could be a double-date with her sister, Mary. Lanny was home from grad school for the weekend, so he and Mary Gomez made up the second couple. Strangely enough, Paul and Linda never dated one another again; however, Mary and Lanny got married.

MARY. Shortly after I met Lanny in May 1974, we went to meet his family. He explained I would also meet his sister who was handicapped with polio. At that time, I was working for an insurance company, and my supervisor had had polio as a child. She had little use of one leg, but otherwise seemed okay. She was the only person I had ever known with polio, so when I met Susan I was taken aback at the severity of her limitations. I was also taken aback at the family itself. I had never before had someone sit down with me and thank God for having me enter their son's life. That was a real shock! I wondered what kind of people these were and what kind of son they had. They were certainly different from anyone I had even known before.

When Lanny left for graduate school again, although quite smitten with Mary, he remembered his dear friend, Bob Coleman, who had not been able to complete his doctorate because of an early marriage and the ensuing responsibilities. Bob had urged Lanny to complete his education before marrying, so Mary and Lanny chose to wait, although by February 1975, they knew they would be married the next year.

Bob also knew Susan, and together the three of them enjoyed many long, philosophical discussions. Bob used these talks to encourage and challenge Lanny by telling Susan she would make a far better physicist than Lanny because he was "too down to earth" to be a theoretical physicist. "Lanny is just destined to become a mundane engineer," he would say, which both complimented Susan and motivated Lanny to strive for a higher goal. Bob's efforts paid off. Lanny became a physicist and only lacked a year of completing his doctorate when he and Mary were married.

MARY. Lanny and I were married at St. Matthews Catholic Church in Arlington. Father Johnson, who had known me nearly all my life, was in charge of the service but was assisted by Lanny's father. This was one of the first joint Catholic-Protestant ceremonies, I believe. I had four bridesmaids with dresses in two shades of blue. Susan's dress was peach-colored, and her mom wore aqua. My mother was in pink. One memory that sticks out with me is that when the four groomsmen entered the church, their shoes sounded like the "Charge of the Light Brigade." I had forgotten how noisy those uncarpeted aisles could be.

The tradition at that time was for the groom to give the bride's mother a rose on their way to the altar and, after the ceremony, for the bride to give the groom's mother a rose. I had decided I would give Susan a rose also because she was the only sibling Lanny had. I had been crying during the ceremony because it was such an emotional time and I thought Susan was seated in the front in the center aisle; but after the ceremony, they had moved her to the aisle between the pew and the

Lanny and Mary taking a cruise in 1996.

window. As I turned to look for her, I forgot I had on a wedding dress and long train and, sure enough, I tripped as I was heading to give her the rose. I could have taken a nasty fall, but Uncle Bernie caught me from behind, so I did not fall; but I saw Susan had tears in her eyes, just as I did in mine. I knew she was pleased that Lanny and I were together, and I knew we would be close friends since we had hit it off from the beginning. I knew Susan and her family loved my mother and sisters as well.

Lanny's father had accepted and already begun his next assignment in North Carolina, and now that Lanny and I were married, his mother and sister would move there, too. Lanny and I moved to Austin for him to finish grad school, so, needless to say, it was hard then for us to visit his family. We would go to North Carolina about once a year, and they would come back to Texas for vacations.

After their marriage, Lanny received his doctorate in physics from the University of Texas at Austin in 1977 and served several years in a postdoctoral position at the government's research labs in Los Alamos, New Mexico. He is currently conducting research under contract with the U.S. Department of Energy in cooperation with the physics department of the University of Texas in Austin. Lanny and Mary have two children, Jennifer Leigh, born July 1979, and Michael Wayne, born February 1983.

CHARLENE. The wedding took place in January 1976. Cecil had been elected to lead the Baptist State Convention of North Carolina in November 1975, and had made several trips back and forth, but we did not consider moving until the festivities were over. By March, the house in Grand Prairie was rented, and we had found a house in Raleigh that met our needs

When Cecil and I came to Raleigh to look for a house, it was the first time I had ever left Susan for more than a few hours. We left her with Cecil's sister, Mary Ruth, and her husband, Bernie. Since Mary Ruth had traveled with us before and had stayed with Susan in the hospital from time to time, I knew she was well able to care for Susan, but I was still anxious. I knew there were a thousand things that might happen that they did not know about. I just wanted to get home to be sure everything was all right.

CECIL. It's easy to see why Charlene felt that so strongly. Susan could have died a hundred times over the years without Charlene's know-how and quick intervention. She could have choked to death—literally! Simple things would cause her to choke, and for a few seconds we would panic, but Charlene was there and took care of it. There were those times when we would be terrified at a particularly bad choking spell, but as soon as it was over, we relaxed. We thought we led a pretty normal life. I guess we trusted, after all these years, that God would help us overcome any dilemma we might face.

CHARLENE. Cecil's call was to serve as General Secretary-Treasurer of the one-million-member Baptist State Convention of North Carolina. This was a fellowship of 3,446 churches with an annual budget of $13 million. This assignment represented a change in location and service for Susan and me, as well as a change in responsibilities for Cecil. Coming to Raleigh had not been an easy decision for us because we were totally immersed in Misión Bautista, and Susan was confident that there she was fulfilling her two callings. In addition, I had somehow gotten the idea that North Carolina Baptists were very liberal. Later, after we had come to know the people, Susan tweaked me by assuring me she had learned there were "more good Baptists in North Carolina than there were people." She was right—the Baptists in North Carolina proved to be among the best.

We found a house in Raleigh with the accessible features we needed to make full use of Susan's equipment. As soon as we were settled in, we set out to find ministries in which we could become involved. It didn't take long. We joined Crabtree Valley Baptist Church and soon were "busy as beavers" there. Susan began writing the history of the church very soon after we arrived, along with several other books. She had already written *The Texas Baptist Way*, *The Florida Baptist Way*, and had coauthored *Oklahoma Baptists Working Together* with Lyle Garlow. In 1979, she began working with Frances Riley to produce *North Carolina Baptists Working Together*. Each of these books pulled together pertinent information about how these individual states worked internally and how they related to the larger Southern Baptist ministries and agencies. For many of the state conventions, these books were the first full-blown attempt to put all these facts and figures together in one publication.

Susan loved children and related to them very well, so it almost went without saying that working with children would be a big part of her ministry in Raleigh. One little girl who attended Susan's classes at Crabtree Valley Church would go home and tell her mother every word Susan had said.

"She is the nicest lady, Mother," the little girl said. "She makes us understand the Bible stories better even than Grandma. She's always smiling and never cross." The mother decided to go meet this nice lady who had so impressed her daughter. When she visited the class, she was

startled to see Susan lying nearly prone in her wheeled chair. The child had never once mentioned that Susan was paralyzed

While Charlene served as Training Union director for the church, Susan worked with the children on Sunday nights, using regular curriculum materials. She also challenged and trained them to participate in Sword Drills, a type of Bible teaching/verse recognition and memorization program for youth that arranges competition between Baptist churches and associations, with an annual state-wide challenge. "Susan's kids" were receptive and enthusiastic, with several receiving associational recognition and at least one going on to state-wide competition.

Crabtree Valley Baptist Church is located in a burgeoning section of Raleigh with a number of large apartment communities close by. Susan and Charlene organized a Big A Club, which met in an apartment complex across from the church. Most of the children who attended this Saturday morning group were not involved in regular church activities, but three youngsters from the complex who began in Big A Club started attending church activities and soon were candidates for baptism. Other children of church member families gave Susan and Charlene much joy as they saw them come to the Lord and accept Him as Savior.

At the same time, Susan volunteered to tutor some young women from South America who were in Raleigh while their husbands studied at North Carolina State University. To her initial surprise, the three ladies were all from Brazil and thus spoke Portuguese, not Spanish. But since Portuguese is close-kin to Spanish, they made out just fine. The situation was made easier, too, by the fact that the last pastor at Misión Bautista in Grand Prairie was a Brazilian who preached in a combination of Spanish, Portuguese, and English. It seems that once again, God was working in Susan's life to enable her to fulfill the ministries He had assigned her. She had truly taken to heart the thrust of WMU, which encourages its members to include missions and witnessing as a continuing part of everyday life.

CHARLENE. About the time we moved to Raleigh, we had a letter from Douglas Waruta, our Kenyan friend, saying he and his family were coming back to the States so he could complete his doctoral work at Southwestern Seminary in Fort Worth. We were delighted at the opportunity to have fellowship with these friends again. When we went back to Texas for visits, we would oftentimes swing by Fort Worth to visit the Warutas, who had added two more sons—Stephen and Joseph—to their family.

When Douglas received his doctorate, the family returned to Africa, this time to Arusha, Tanzania, where Douglas became president of our

East Africa Baptist Theological Seminary. Years earlier, he had been the first graduate of the seminary there; now he would serve as its head. Douglas is living proof that Southern Baptist investment in overseas missions pays rich dividends in changed lives which are reinvested in the work of the Kingdom.

Susan carried on regular correspondence with Douglas and his family for years. She wrote and, with the help of the Texas Baptist Convention, produced a widely used filmstrip on Baptist work in East Africa, using the notes, pictures, and sound recordings her father had gathered while on mission trips there.

CECIL. One of the worst scares we had with Susan was when we were still living in Raleigh. I was to speak at Fort Worth, so Charlene and Susan decided to go along and stop in San Angelo for a visit with Charlene's dad, who was ill. Susan had developed a slight cold, a condition which was never taken lightly since she could not cough or clear her breathing passages effectively. She seemed to be doing better, so we began the trip in high spirits.

By the time we reached Cleburn, Texas, Susan was much worse. Usually she was game to keep on, but this time she told us, "We'll have to stop. I'm too sick to go on." I reluctantly made arrangements to leave them in the motel there, unloaded, set up Susan's equipment, and hurriedly left to keep my engagement. Motel management was quite concerned and made arrangements next day to move Susan, Charlene, and all Susan's equipment into a larger room. Charlene struggled to control the congestion that was choking Susan's throat and chest. This was not pneumonia. For anyone else, it would simply have been a bad cold, but for Susan, it spelled trouble. At one point, an emergency medical team was even called in to help clear her of congestion.

I hurried back as soon as I could get away, but Susan was still too sick even to return home. Our plans to visit Charlene's father were, of course, abandoned. After five or six days in the motel, we started home but Susan continued to worsen. By the time we arrived in Raleigh, she could scarcely breathe. Once again, we faced the very real possibility that Susan would not be able to throw off this illness. "It's not time, yet, Father," we prayed. "Please, not yet." We realized she was going to need specialized help we weren't equipped to give her, so we took Susan to Rex Hospital in Raleigh. They discovered she was experiencing bronchial spasms which could be controlled with a medicated inhaler. Almost immediately, her symptoms cleared. With relief, we knew the Father had answered our plea. The time was not yet.

Susan believed Christian stewardship included the wise use of the earth's resources and was aware that much of the world's famine and disease comes from the abuse of God's gifts. She deplored waste and looked for ways both she and her family could "make do" with less. During their ten years in Raleigh, Susan developed many of these environmental interests and devoted much of her time, energy, and money to promoting them for the rest of her adult life.

When the energy crunch hit the country in the late 1970s, she set out to educate herself concerning energy conservation. It seemed then that the nation was in for a long siege of energy restrictions, and she wanted to be involved in finding some answers. As usual, she turned to Lanny to learn more about the problem.

LANNY. Considering her handicaps, it would seem that Susan would have had a lot of free time on her hands, but she stayed busy with projects, writing, and reading. I envied her ability to deal with her limitations and still stay on top of so many subjects. She was a source of information to the entire family. Items and issues would come up on the news, and we would often wonder "what's behind that?" and Susan would already know or would dig up the information and fill us in. My interests were in math and science. While Susan was not a scientist, she was such a broad thinker in so many areas that there was really nothing that did not interest her. As I began to learn about astronomy and physics and science in general, she became interested in them, too, as a way to satisfy her own insatiable thirst for knowledge.

It's often been stated that if you're really good at science, you can explain it to your grandmother. I guess I'm something of a teacher at heart, because I always enjoyed the chance to explain things to Susan. If we can't succeed at explaining what we're doing—some simple concept or theory—then we're failing at one of our missions, which is to educate and help other people share in the joy of studying nature and figuring out physical laws and processes. The times I spent in exploring these things with Susan will always be a fond part of my remembering.

Susan's interest in energy conservation stemmed from her concern for the wise use of God's gifts to mankind. She knew she needed to learn all about alternate sources of energy, as well as techniques for conserving the energy sources we already had, so she would pick my brain to learn all she could. She had read a great deal about power plants and about how much waste heat they throw away, and she felt this was due to negligence and carelessness on their part. I assured her there were some basic laws one couldn't beat no matter how hard one tried. This Second Law of

Thermodynamics was one of them. There simply is no way of conserving all the energy power plants produce. She then turned her attention to seeking ways that churches and individuals could cut back on overall use of energy supplies. To her, all this was a natural part of missions.

CHARLENE. After Susan felt "sort of" qualified, she volunteered her services to the Raleigh Baptist Association and its one hundred churches as an energy consultant. She conducted a conference on energy conservation at an associational meeting and, with the help of Beth, a Meredith College student who served as chauffeur and "loader," she toured a number of churches in the area. Armed with a thermometer and light meter, she and Beth took readings throughout the various church facilities and determined if they were overlighted or overheated, and then suggested any changes needed.

Conservation in general became an abiding concern for Susan, but by far her overriding interest in those days was the plight of itinerant farm workers, whose cause was championed by the Farm Workers Union. She sought, and usually received, permission from local churches to put up posters in support of Cesar Chavez and his farm workers in California. In our home, although grapes were among her favorite fruits, we boycotted them for years.

Susan was also very conscious of the plight of the Hispanic migrant workers who came into our country annually to harvest our crops. Of course, she had been quite involved in Hispanic ministries in Texas, but this was different. She learned that North Carolina played host each summer to literally tens of thousands of migrants who made a broad sweep across the southern states to plant and harvest crops. These workers usually brought their families, traveling in rusty old cars and buses, and living in primitive migrant camps dotted across the state. Beginning in late January in Florida, they harvested vegetables, then crept northward to plant tobacco and later to harvest vegetables and apples in the fall. Their children were educated in short bursts, moving maybe three or four times each school year, then working in the hot sun alongside their families in the fields all summer. Making a small but needed contribution to the meager family income, they hardly knew what childhood was.

Each year when our church filled small plastic bags with soap, washcloths, toothpaste, toothbrushes, and other personal items for these seasonal workers, Susan helped by avidly promoting the project as well as helping fund the purchases. This was, once again, a way for her to serve her beloved Hispanic people.

11

A Broadened View of Missions

Susan's concept of missions included a variety of causes. Her Christian faith included the totality of life. She was concerned about global problems such as pollution, the overuse of chemicals in agriculture, and the waste of natural resources. She was a committed member of organizations such as Friends of the Earth, the Nature Conservancy, and the American Farmland Trust.

Susan was also a card-carrying Democrat and was interested in and served as an activist for a number of political concerns. To her, it was important to have a voice in governmental policies—more important to take part than which side one chose. She thought nothing of calling her representatives and senators, even the president! Of course, she almost always had to talk with someone in their offices, but she let her ideas and opinions be known. She was a member of Operation Vote Smart and never missed an opportunity to vote. If the weather prohibited her from getting into the polls, some kind person there would bring her ballot out to the car so she could express her convictions properly.

CHARLENE. Susan was also a strong supporter of programs to help others less fortunate. She donated regularly to the Salvation Army, United Way, Habitat for Humanity, American Red Cross, Humane Society, Public Citizen, and The Caring Place, a local help agency providing food, clothing, furniture, and job assistance for the needy. But uppermost among Susan's good causes were her church and Baptist work all over the world. Though most of her gifts were small in amount, they were large, percentage-wise. Since Susan lived at home and was not responsible for food, shelter, and clothing, she was able to use the income she generated from her writing as she chose. She delighted in giving and sometimes even wrote her own checks. She kept her own financial records, computing and setting aside 15 percent for her church and

10 percent for other good causes each month. Her largest gifts were to the Hispanic Baptist Theological Seminary in San Antonio, Texas, reflecting her continuing love for Hispanic missions. This ongoing commitment to her calling was reflected in her will, which provided for seventy percent of her assets to be shared among the Texas Baptist Cooperative Program, the Hispanic Baptist Theological Seminary, and the Gazette International Networking Institute which serves persons with respiratory paralysis.

MARY. Susan was always full of enthusiasm. She had a different way of looking at life and at her limitations. One time when we visited in Raleigh, Susan greeted us with what to her was a great idea. "You've just got to meet this new friend I have. She's so neat and rejuvenating!" Susan went on to explain that her friend had a physical handicap, which I don't remember, but I do remember that when she came in, she was the bounciest little thing I'd ever seen. She was very short—almost dwarf-like. Her arms were very short, with her hands attached near her shoulders. She had driven over to Susan's in her specially-equipped car.

They talked excitedly about how she and Susan wanted to be independent and to fend for themselves. Susan wanted Lanny and me to talk their parents into letting them move in together in an apartment of their own. We asked how they thought they could manage that, knowing it would not be feasible, but Susan, who was always a bit of a rebel, was also the most independent, dependent person I've ever known. She assured us that, with the help of her friend, they could manage quite well. Susan urged us to help them, saying, "I know Mama won't go for it, but I want you to know this is what we are talking about." You could tell they were excited, but mainly they were keen on the possibilities of independent living.

One time, the family went to Washington, D.C., to do some sightseeing. When we got to the Lincoln Memorial, Susan decided she had to get up that long flight of steps to see Abraham Lincoln up close. At that time, they had no entrances, ramps, elevators, nothing for handicapped persons—but she was so determined to see it all that I took the respirator, Mamaw took her bag and all our purses, and Lanny and Papaw decided they would lift Susan up those steps, pausing to rest on the landings. I had thought I would get off easy with the respirator, but no. That thing was heavy! It looked about the size of an overnight case, but it had the weight of I don't know what. I rested every time the guys took a rest, and, hard as it was, it was really nice that Susan could read the words and see everything up close for herself.

Soon after that, we went to Mount Vernon and toured George Washington's house. There you could go up to the top level, but the authorities did not want to take responsibility for Susan's going up even though there was an elevator. Papaw assured them that he would sign any paper they wished to release them of any liability because Susan wanted to go so badly. This was another encounter with Susan's determination—a determination that came from deep inside and shot out to everybody she met. It was just like a ray of light shooting out.

The first time we took Jennifer to North Carolina, Lanny had been away on a business trip in that direction, and I was flying in from New Mexico. Jennifer was around three months old and would be meeting her grandparents for the first time. I was traveling alone and was loaded down with a car seat, diaper bag, purse, and an overnight bag in case our luggage got lost. As we left the plane, I asked several people to take a picture of Jennifer meeting her grandparents, but everybody I asked refused. So now, to my sorrow, we do not have a picture of that first meeting.

At that time, airports did not have the boarding ramps like today. Instead, they rolled out a portable set of steps right up to the plane door. Papaw somehow got through the security and came right up those steps to help me out. He took Jennifer, who was still in her car seat, and I took the rest. I had been dreading coming down those steep steps, but Papaw just took over and almost immediately we were in the car which was parked close by. I knew he must have gotten there very early to have found a parking space so near. We drove to the house and found that Susan and Mamaw had gotten together with neighbors and church friends who had loaned them all kinds of baby furniture. Susan got such a kick out of my expression when I walked in and saw a crib and playpen, and even a high chair. We had mentioned it briefly on the phone, but I didn't think they would do that much.

Several years later, we went to North Carolina for Christmas. Mamaw had told me earlier that Santa Claus was not something they emphasized at Christmas. I had replied that we were so poor growing up, we didn't have any Santa Claus around, but that, hopefully, my children were going to be raised a little differently. When I arrived, I had brought stockings and the whole "smear," and though Michael was too little at that time to know what was going on, Jennifer was old enough to realize something special should be happening.

Now, Susan always had the ability to be a good mediator. She just instinctively knew how to help each party understand both sides. She could always come to me and explain anything so I could understand completely. She had told me, "Mary, just suggest it real strongly and they'll go along." So I explained to Lanny's parents that if they didn't want to do this, it was fine. "Just wake me up early and I'll do the stocking thing," I said. Susan spoke up and said, "Oh, I'm the first one up, I can do it!" Of course we all knew it was impossible for her to do this herself. Sure enough, next morning I didn't have to do anything. Those stockings were pinned up and filled and ready. I just wish the kids had been old enough to appreciate it.

CHARLENE. Susan never made a distinction between her beliefs as a Christian and the issues of everyday life. To her, they were one and the same. One of her most avid interests was in handgun control. She was involved in an ongoing debate by letter with Texas Senator Jim Turner concerning pending legislation on this issue. She was also deeply committed to citizen participation in the conservation of natural resources, and in political issues such as the Center for National Independence in Politics. For years she had carried on a continuing correspondence with Ralph Nader about the various issues they both championed, and when she had the opportunity to meet him in person, at a Houston conference, she considered it one of the big moments in her life. Her sign, "Public Citizen—Nader's Raiders. Fighting for Better Government and Public Safety," graced her desk. When someone would see and ask about it, Susan took the opportunity to share her convictions on the various issues.

Susan may have thought her parents were sometimes too strict with her, but she never argued or openly defied their decisions. She displayed anger only a few times, but no one who faced her displeasure ever doubted her ability to express herself with clarity and force. One incident involved a time when the Rays received notice that Medicare had purchased the humidifier she used with her positive pressure ventilator. It seems that Medicare would rent some types of equipment from a dealer only for a certain period of time, after which it would purchase the equipment. The snag was that Medicare had paid full price to Lifecare for a humidifier that Susan had used for over five years. Cecil was going to call Lifecare, but Susan protested. "You may get mad. Let me call." When she did, she asked for the president of the company. As she explained her concern, her face became redder and redder. She protested that they had not been notified of the changeover and that it was unfair to charge Medicare the full purchase price for used equipment. "If you charge for a new one, I want a new one," she said. The company president agreed, and she received a new humidifier. Later, she and the company president became friends of a sort when he assisted her with information for an article she wrote, "The High Cost of Things Medical."

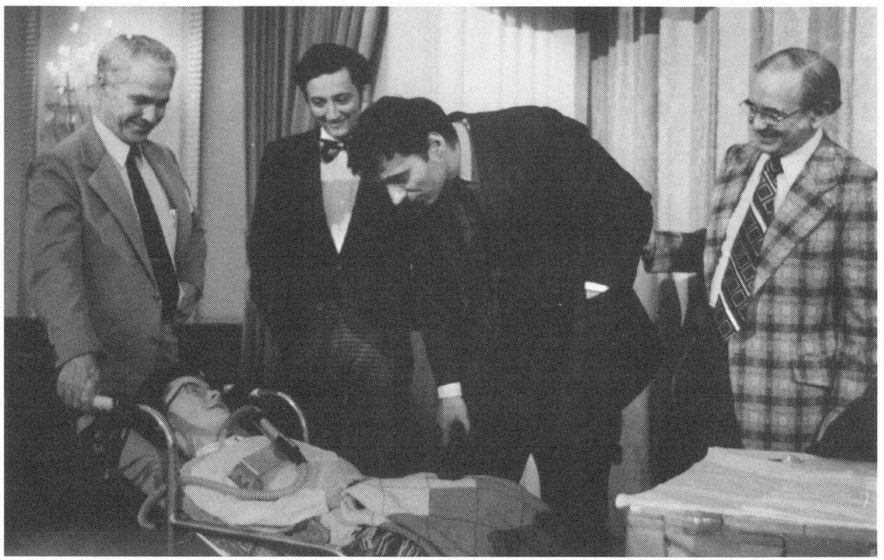

Susan chatted with Ralph Nader at a Christian Life Seminar in Houston. Nader heard from Susan frequently over the years. Shown also are (left to right) her father, Cecil Ray, and Walton Gaddy and Foy Valentine of the Southern Baptist Christian Life Commission.

Eventually, these high costs Susan wrote about became a point of controversy between the Rays and the medical supply company. For twenty-five years, with help from Medicare and the Rays' private insurance, they had rented two positive pressure ventilators, but these units were getting old and more trouble-prone. Although the company was able to keep them running and was prompt in shipping replacement parts, over the years monthly fees had grown to six hundred dollars.

Suddenly, the Rays received notice that the new monthly fees would be over thirteen hundred dollars. Again, neither Medicare nor the Rays' insurance company protested, but the Rays did. They notified the company that the new fees were not acceptable. This time the company made no adjustments, but the Rays would not give in.

Cecil had been experimenting with building a positive pressure ventilator before this occurred, but without success. The major obstacle was in finding a suitable electric motor that would fit into the limited space needed to keep the unit practical for Susan's use. He had completed a positive pressure unit which could be used in the van and would operate on the twelve-volt dc power from the van's battery. Using this test unit for Susan in travel, Cecil was able to determine that the piston-drive system would be both workable and satisfactory for respiratory assistance. About this time, manufacturers came out with several new gear motors, both ac and dc , which, with a converter, made them ideal for the ventilator units. After building an at-home ac unit and testing it for two months, Cecil built two stand-by ac units and a twelve-volt dc unit for travel which could use a small battery such as those in riding lawn mowers. They discovered this unit could be battery operated for up to thirty-two hours before recharging. After completing the first unit, the Rays returned one of Susan's leased units and, as the other units were completed and well-tested, they returned the other rented unit and notified both their insurance company and Medicare. When charges for this discontinued equipment were still received the next month, they notified both the insurance company and Medicare, which had continued to make payments. The Rays also requested the company to refund fees. This was done without comment from any party. A few months later, the equipment company president called Susan to ask how she was getting along with her article, "The High Cost of Things Medical." He also asked how the equipment her father had built was working. "Just fine," she answered to both questions.

He continued, "Well, I guess you miss having the automatic sigh breath feature, don't you?" She replied, "Oh, no! We have this feature on our units also!"

CHARLENE. In September 1983, Cecil was elected National Director of Planned Growth in Giving by the Southern Baptist Convention Executive Committee; however, he did not assume this post until January 1984. His assignment was to lead Southern Baptists to give $20 billion dollars a year, and to increase church giving through the Cooperative Program by $2.5 billion by the year 2000. These goals were to provide funding for the ambitious programs of Bold Mission Thrust, a plan adopted by Southern Baptists to give every person on earth an opportunity to hear the gospel before the turn of the century. Unfortunately, a power struggle between two factions in Southern Baptist life may have sounded the death knell for this dream.

We continued to live in Raleigh as Susan and Cecil worked together in formulating this new stewardship challenge, which delighted Susan since it fitted right in with her love of missions. Together they wrote the book *Cooperation, the Baptist Way to a Lost World*.

In June 1985, we moved our travel trailer onto a lot we had bought for a new home in Georgetown, Texas. We chose this location because it was about twenty miles from Lanny and his family in Austin. Cecil hired contractors to lay the foundation, sidewalks, and garage floor. Then he secured others to frame up, close in, and roof the house. The interior of the garage and adjoining workshop were finished and equipped to live in. The rest was to be done by Cecil after we had moved in and gotten settled, but, for now, the interior of the house remained unfinished.

MARY. We were delighted to have the family back close again. It meant we could visit more often and the children could spend time with Susan and their grandparents more frequently. In the summer of 1985, Lanny made a trip to Germany, and I wanted to go with him. Since Mamaw, Papaw, and Susan had moved back to Texas in their travel trailer to start their new home in Georgetown, they offered to stay with the children while we were gone.

Now Susan was always thoughtful in ways you'd never expect. One night before we left, as Susan and I were outside looking at the stars and waiting for everyone to complete their showers, she said, "You know, Mary, we'll soon be moving into our house, and it's not very far away. You're going to have to let us know if we get too close or interfere with your family in any way. We'll back off, because we really don't want to interfere, but you'll have to let us know." And never once did they interfere. They never have, and we've been married twenty years. Our two families have done many things together, with my mother and sisters and Lanny's family taking turns having Christmas at one another's homes. We have enjoyed a close relationship over the years.

It was sometimes easy to forget that Susan dealt with problems we never faced. One Christmas after they moved back, I decided to make a chocolate cake with white icing—white icing like peaks of snow, according to the picture that illustrated the recipe. None of us was good at baking, but Susan watched and encouraged me as I started mixing the batter. I read the recipe and asked Susan, "How am I supposed to know when this icing 'peaks'"?

Susan answered, "I don't know, Mary, maybe it should hit a high note!"

I don't know why it seemed so funny, but we started laughing. Mamaw came in and began explaining the definition of terms in that cookbook. By now, I was totally frustrated with that recipe, but the more frustrated I got, the more we laughed. Now when one of us laughs that hard, we might get choked and then get over it, but in Susan's situation, when she got choked, you had to react quickly. Mamaw called out, "Hurry! Get me some water!" I knew I had to act fast but I couldn't move. It seemed like I was rooted to the spot. We finally got things right again, but it was quite scary and served to remind me once again of how careful we had to be with Susan.

CHARLENE. After we moved to Georgetown, Jennifer and Michael began coming to our house for sleepovers. Susan became their sitter and chief source of entertainment. She would put her projects aside and devote herself fully to them. It is doubtful that, until the last few years, they were even aware that she had a full day of work and activities to keep her busy. One of their favorite games was "hospital," with Susan the patient—perhaps in more ways than one. Poor thing, she had diseases of both humans and animals.

MICHAEL. What I remember best is Susan playing with us: checkers, Wheel of Fortune, and lots of other games. We read Bible stories and had long talks about them and about a lot of other stuff. She would spend lots of time watching me put together model cars and airplanes. Our best fun was when we played doctor and nurse with Susan, 'cause she would lay there and Jenny would draw pictures of bad diseases and say, "This is what you have in your stomach," and Susan would say, "Oh, no!" and we would have to operate. That's what I remember best.

JENNIFER. I remember little things, like taking pictures of the bluebonnets which she loved. I seldom thought of Susan as my aunt; I always thought of her as one of my best friends. When we went for a visit with our grandparents, our first question was, "Where is Susan? Is she sick?" Then I'd go straight in and make her an appointment with the doctor—me. We'd get sheets from her doll bed and use them as her hospital gown. I'd give her a checkup and discover she had heart worms. I was usually Dr. Ray and Michael was my nurse, but sometimes we'd alternate roles. She always came through the surgery okay, but the next checkup would show she had mysteriously developed another worm and we'd go to work again.

What seems interesting to me now is that even as a young girl, I never thought of Susan as having polio and being restricted to a chair and a machine that breathed for her. In my eyes, she was just like anyone else, and there were no limits to what she could do. Of course, her movements were limited, but her spirit and enthusiasm were not. She was always fun to be with.

Nighttime is what I looked forward to most with Susan. Michael and I would help get Susan in her iron lung, and then we would sleep together beside her in her single bed, that is until we got too big to both fit in. Michael usually fell asleep pretty fast and that's when Susan and I really had some good talks. We talked about everything, and she would listen to my questions and problems just like they were her own. It was better than a slumber party.

One time, when I was kind of little, I was going through her drawers and found a clip with purple stones. I thought it was pretty, so I took it. When I was found out, Susan didn't even seem mad at me. I was so scared that she'd be mad at me, but she just asked for it quietly and thanked me politely when I gave it back. That was the only misunderstanding we ever had, and it taught me a lot.

MARY. At that time, Jennifer was enrolled at Sanchez Elementary School, which was pretty much divided between Anglo and Hispanic students. With Jennifer being half Hispanic, we thought the school would give her a good opportunity to learn the language and to appreciate her culture. One day, Jennifer came home with a worksheet which had some words I could not figure out. The truth is, if I took a course in Spanish, I would have to start with Spanish 101. I know colloquial Spanish, but not the formal usage, so I called the Rays to see if Susan could help.

I talked to Papaw, who immediately handed the phone to Mamaw, who helped a little but soon was stumped, so she put Susan on the phone. How good was Susan's Spanish? Let's just say that Jennifer made 100.

Another thing I remember about Susan is her ability to play games well. She loved them. One night when Lanny and I came to visit, we became bored with television and got out the Scrabble game. I learned very quickly I'd better get out or be brought to shame, so I baled out. Lanny and Susan then started to really get into it, and Susan was beating Lanny badly. Now I always think Lanny is the most intelligent person I know, so all of a sudden, I saw Susan in a different light. She was coming up with words I'd never even heard of. Lanny began to challenge her, so I had to go get a dictionary. Susan would spell the words, I'd look them up, and, sure enough, she was right every time

Lanny knew he was losing, and he doesn't like to lose at games, so he pulled out his ace-in-the-hole. Out came his physics terms, and his calculus terms, and his car mechanics terms. When Susan challenged him, his words were not in the dictionary, so Susan won the game. Mainly she won because Lanny could not substantiate his words, but I got a real kick out of that because Lanny finally got beaten.

JENNIFER. Aunt Susan was always there for me—for all of us. If I needed help with my writing, I would call her. If I needed help with a problem or just someone to talk to, she was there. When we'd go out to dinner, people would stare at her, but she was just like you and me in my eyes. I was always very proud when she came with my grandparents to my school functions.

Aunt Susan never met a stranger. One Christmas I brought a boyfriend over to meet her, and she just opened up and talked away, which put him at ease from the beginning. All of my friends enjoyed being with her; she got along with everyone, no matter what sex, color, or religion.

My only regret is that Aunt Susan never got to see me dance in my last contest. The morning of her death was also the morning of my dance contest. Even though she had passed away, I still participated because I thought she would want me to. It was the hardest and the longest day of my life. At first, I got pretty emotional and thought I couldn't do it, but I got myself together and told my friends, "I will dance this one for Susan." Now, whenever I perform, in my heart I dedicate my hard work and accomplishments to her. She is still an inspiration to me, and, out of everyone I know, she is the one I always looked up to and always will.

12

Confined but Unfettered

CECIL. Planned Growth in Giving was to provide Susan with her greatest opportunity to share her convictions with others. Surprisingly, public speaking eventually became a part of that ministry. Although she had a number of opportunities to speak to large audiences, Susan never considered herself a good speaker. Of course, her greatest number of speaking/teaching opportunities involved her participation in all phases of her churches' programs, but there were other opportunities as well.

Before our move to North Carolina, Susan had written a book entitled *The Baptist Way*, which gave a broad picture of Baptist polity in Texas and in the Southern Baptist Convention, and explained how Texas Baptists work together through these two conventions. She was asked to speak at the State Missions Commission of the Baptist General Convention of Texas about the book, which was to serve as an introduction to the fiftieth anniversary of the Cooperative Program. Since she had assisted me through the years in developing Cooperative Program material, she was well prepared for the task.

Another well-received address Susan gave was to the annual meeting of the Baptist State Convention of North Carolina. That program featured the special ministries of several people who were actively serving Christ in spite of physical handicaps. Later, as a result of her contribution to developing the Planned Growth in Giving concept, she was asked to speak at a meeting of Key Leadership officers at First Baptist Church in Nashville, where she shared her enthusiasm for mission outreach with nearly six hundred denominational leaders. It was a rewarding experience for her and an inspiring one for those who heard her, so inspiring in fact, that some of them suggested she present the same message to a larger audience—the Southern Baptist Convention's annual meeting that year in Dallas. Prior to her speech to the full convention, she stopped off in Nashville to speak to the staff of the Sunday School Board as well.

Susan knew how to present her case. She had methodically set herself to the task, preparing herself with facts, figures, and illustrations of what Planned Growth in Giving could mean to world evangelism. She combined the urgency of embracing Planned Growth in Giving with a clear chiding of Baptists for allowing controversy to destroy "our greatest opportunity to win the world for Christ." In spite of her chiding, she received multiple standing ovations from the huge crowd for her speech.

In past years, attendance at the annual meeting of the Southern Baptist Convention had been as many as twenty-five thousand, but as Susan prepared herself to address such a gathering, estimates of attendance climbed to almost forty-five thousand—enough to make the most seasoned public speaker tremble at the thought of looking out over that sea of faces. Yet she was determined to make the most of this opportunity.

Of all the challenges and opportunities Susan faced and conquered in fulfilling her ministry, perhaps the most difficult was that of public speaking. Standing before groups of people to share one's thoughts and convictions is seldom easy for anyone. Even persons who are trained to do so find themselves "quaking in their boots," so Susan certainly could not have been faulted had she refused such a challenge by claiming her handicaps. But that was not Susan's way.

Her voice was not very strong; indeed her voice was very soft, and punctuated with pauses as her unit pumped air into her lungs so she could project her words. She could not stand, gripping the podium for courage as she delivered her speech. She could not make use of notes, there was no place to lay them. Lying at an angle as she did, she could not even see all of her audience at one time, yet she took every challenge offered to her, seeing each one as an opportunity to make others aware of the causes she believed in so strongly. In fact, Susan might have been a bit indignant had she been commended for accepting the challenge of public speaking. She had insisted, over and over throughout her life, that she was not different in what things she did, only in the way she did them.

"A missionary is one sent to tell others what they have experienced firsthand with the Lord," she might have said. "I can certainly do that!"

CHARLENE. Preparing for that speech must have been harrowing for Susan although, on the surface, she appeared calm. Cecil had developed the concept for Planned Growth in Giving, and, like all the equipment he had designed and built for Susan, every aspect of the plan had been carefully designed and tested in his own family. The concept was simple but quite different from traditional stewardship promotions. Most Christian leaders have always promoted the idea of tithing—that is, giving one-tenth of one's income to the Lord through one's church. There is strong biblical support for this concept; however, Cecil saw two basic weaknesses in this approach in today's world.

First, many families were unable to free up a full 10 percent without careful long-range planning because of standing commitments. Second, some folks were quite able to give more than the tithe but had not yet reached a level of commitment that would challenge them to do so. Buying into the concept of Planned Growth in Giving would combat both of these problems, because families were being challenged to take a new look at where they were currently in their giving, where they would like to be in five to ten years, and then commit themselves to increase their giving gradually but consistently each year until they had reached their stated goals.

Although Susan did not have a great deal of personal income, she adopted Planned Growth in Giving just like the rest of the family. She tried it, she liked it, and she became one of its most enthusiastic followers. When the opportunity came to speak on the program in Nashville to leadership from thirty-four state Baptist conventions, she thought of the stature and influence of these leaders, gulped once or twice, and said, "If they want me and it will help, I'll do it." This was also her attitude when she was later asked to make that same presentation to the annual national convention in Dallas.

For years, the Southern Baptist Convention had used huge magnification screens to enable the large audiences to more easily see those who spoke from the platform and those who came to the microphones to raise questions or to address issues under discussion. The night Susan spoke, tens of thousands of people were packed into the main auditorium and into satellite rooms set up to accommodate the overflow. They looked up on those giant screens and saw Susan, seated in her wheeled chair, waiting for the auditorium to grow quiet. As she began to explain and challenge them to adopt Planned Growth in Giving, they sensed her faith, her commitment, and the spiritual logic of what she was asking them to do.

Susan did not mention her handicaps or seek their pity. Such an idea would have had her sputtering with indignation. Rather, she simply talked with them as one Christian to another about their journey in the faith. There was both humor and logic in what she said, but there was more. There was the clear challenge to each of them to try Planned Growth in Giving in their own lives, and it came from one who shamed them when they compared their commitment to hers.

Susan was wheeled away from the mikes and cameras to a thunderous ovation from a vast audience, many of whom she could not even see. Her attitude about it all? Not "Boy, I wowed them tonight," but "That wasn't as bad as I expected. What else can I do to help?"

In speaking to this mass audience, Susan had reached more people with her mission message than she might have had she served in a traditional missionary appointment for a lifetime. In every sense of the term, she was a "missionary extraordinaire."

By 1988, Cecil was only working part-time at his stewardship task for the Southern Baptist Convention Executive Committee and took full retirement in 1989 after serving Southern Baptists for forty-eight years. A Resolution of Appreciation was presented to him during the annual Southern Baptist Convention meeting in Las Vegas in 1989. This did not mean retirement from Christian service, however. The family has continued to serve faithfully through their local church and association.

CECIL. Susan never forgot any facts and characteristics she learned about polio and its effects. She never seemed to fret about her condition; she was just eternally optimistic. She dealt with scoliosis as a side effect of her paralysis and for years could not be propped to sit straighter than a 35–40 degree angle. She remembered that as a child she had seen, on a checkup visit to Houston, a human spine attached to a gooseneck lamp and had heard Dr. Paul Harrington explain that his dream was to straighten crooked backs without the trauma of fusion just by putting a metal rod alongside the spine. Years later, she decided to explore this option for her own use, but it was not to be. While we were in North Carolina, she read that a doctor at Duke Hospital had developed a device, similar to the heart pacemaker, that could be implanted in patients with phrenic nerve damage. It could stimulate and reactivate muscle action and enable the patient to breathe. She immediately called and asked if this would work for her. The doctor was doubtful, but at her insistence agreed to see her, so we made the trip to Duke.

As always, Susan became the subject of great interest to other doctors and interns at Duke. Each day, several came by to look at Susan and her breathing equipment. They had seen pictures of an iron lung and had studied the devastating effects of polio, but had never seen a respiratory polio patient. One doctor in particular was intrigued by Susan's skill in "frog breathing." He would place his hand on her stomach and note the amount of air she could inhale by that method. He was quick to recognize that Susan's ability was a marvel—or as we had gradually come to see—God's unique gift to Susan that enabled her to live and be productive.

This trip, however, did not produce our hoped-for results. Since Susan's phrenic nerve had been so badly damaged for so long, it did not respond to the new stimulator at all.

CHARLENE. Another aspect of Susan's condition that was of interest to the doctors at Duke was the fact that she had never had a pressure or bed sore. This condition, which is a result of lying prone over long periods of time, is quite common among paralyzed patients, but we never had to deal with it. For one thing, Susan slept on her sides at night, rarely ever on her back. In fact, when she had a cold, we had to turn her every hour or two to prevent drainage from her bronchial tubes from seeping into her lungs. Even on a normal night, she would call for us once or twice to turn her to her other side.

Word spread quickly among the medical students at Duke, and Susan became a celebrity. When one of the students would see us in the hall, he would exclaim, "Oh, you're the one I've heard about who's never had a bed sore!"

People who became aware of Susan's writing ability often asked how she could do her study and research, make notes, and write materials ready for release. They read her writings, wondering how she knew and understood all that was required. No one, except her parents, understood how educated Susan really was. She read and studied continually, thirsty to learn about everything.

The best explanation is that Susan never ceased being a student. She read enough to stay informed in a variety of areas: Texas politics, political and social issues faced in America and around the world, current events, history, archaeology, and many other areas. She had strong opinions and convictions on what was happening and did not hesitate to write company officials, legislators, and even the president if the subject warranted. Her crusades grew out of her quest for knowledge and her concern for fairness and equality.

CHARLENE. Susan became fond of big words very early in life, and by the time she was or eight or nine, she could use them fairly well. Once when she watched as one of Lanny's building projects came tumbling down, she admonished, "Lanny, if you would attend to your affairs in a more orderly manner, you would not encounter such occurrences!" When she first began writing for the Sunday School Board as an adult, she was dismayed to learn that a writer is encouraged to write at an eighth-grade level.

*Except for two articles published in the **Baptist Student** magazine, one on spoonerizing and one about controlling the weather, Susan's writing* *was not humorous. Not that she was long-faced; she had a puckish sense of humor, probably inherited from her mother. They loved to be silly together, often playing pranks on unsuspecting family and friends. For her last Halloween social, with her Sunday School department, Charlene was "Madam Lazonga" and Susan was "Tyrola, the Mysterious." They performed many mystifying feats and were decidedly goofy.*

CHARLENE. Susan, the wheelchair archeologist, was never able to do any active participation in on-site explorations, but she was quite knowledgable concerning worldwide discoveries. Her only firsthand thrill came when we carried her to the Williamson County dig in 1994. There she watched entranced as archeologists exhumed and examined real specimens of Stone Age Indian artifacts.

She was particularly interested in the Dead Sea Scrolls and the ruins of the Old Temple in Jerusalem, and read extensively in these areas. She wrote a few articles on these subjects as well. One of her last freelance articles, entitled "Moses' Dream of a Perfect Society," dealt with the strong similarities between modern concepts of society and hygiene and those set forth in the Mosaic law. It was accepted and published in a periodical for Bible teachers.

Another of Susan's writing efforts was included in the *Antologia de Dramas*, a compilation of Christmas dramas in Spanish. Every year while we were in Grand Prairie, there was a different Christmas pageant presented at Misión Bautista. Many of them were written by Susan and me. I would stage and direct them with Susan watching to catch any detail I might have missed.

A few years ago, when Susan read of a contest the Baptist Spanish Publishing House in El Paso was conducting, she had me enter "Vino El Salvador," one of our earlier scripts. My stage directions were in English, so she had to translate them with the help of a Mexican friend. She had originally written the dialogue using her Spanish Bible, so it was soon ready to go. We won second place in the contest. I'm just sorry it took so long to publish the book. Susan didn't get to see it in print.

CECIL. Susan never woke up with nothing to do that day. She spent some time every Sunday afternoon planning her week ahead. Her interests were broad and her involvements, though physically limited, were many. The telephone and typewriter were her bridges to the world, and she kept them going for much of her day. She regularly read the publications from all the causes she contributed to. In addition, she read the monthly magazines, *Discover* and *Biblical Archaeology Review*, and completed ten volumes of the Time-Life series, *Time Frame*, which dealt with history from 3000 B.C. to A.D. 1300. She felt she had pretty well covered the events after that in her schoolwork.

CHARLENE. We have often been asked if Susan felt left out of so many of life's opportunities. She may have, but she never expressed this to any of us. She sometimes did express frustration, but it was to argue that she could do things when we displayed caution. This, however, was due more to her adventuresome and crusading spirit rather than to a feeling of being left out.

CECIL. I think there were times when Susan felt her mother was too strict on her. After all, she was an adult, but we just didn't trust her to go off with many people. There were simply too many things that could happen with someone who was not accustomed to caring for her. I don't think, however, that Susan ever showed any signs of not knowing she was fortunate to have a family who cared for her. There were times, of course, when she would have liked to challenge us about something we didn't let her do. I saw resignation on her face on several occasions when she really wanted to do something, but I never saw resentment. To be as superbly practical as Susan was, she still had the independent streak that any normal person has.

CHARLENE. In the years after we moved back to Texas, we renewed many of the friendships that had been so meaningful when our children were small. One was with Cheryl Dorton, who had been a best childhood friend of Susan's when we lived in San Antonio. Cheryl had even named one of her little girls after Susan. During one of our trips to their home, Susan had promised little Susan a trip to the Tower of the Americas in San Antonio and to buy her dinner there. Arrangements were made for little Susan's family to be our guests at a noon meal. Both Susans had a great time seeing San Antonio from the revolving dining area of the tower and thoroughly enjoyed their day

Another renewal of old friendships occurred in 1993 when James, the oldest son of Mary and Douglas Waruta, came to the states to attend Hardin-Simmons University. The Rays, along with some of those who sponsored his father, are now helping James with finances. He spent his first Thanksgiving and two weeks that first Christmas with the Rays at their home in Georgetown. When James's brother, Ben, came to Hardin-Simmons in the fall of 1995, this same group undertook to assist him as well. Like their father, both of these are bright and dedicated young men and will be a great asset when they return to assume leadership positions in their country.

CHARLENE. When we moved to Georgetown, Susan began looking for ways to fulfill her calling to serve in missions. She soon became deeply involved in the work of Baptist Women, where one of her pet projects was the formation of a Missions Intercessory Telephone Prayer Chain. Her idea for this ministry came to her while serving as enlistment/enlargement director for the Crestview Baptist WMU. The church already had an intercessory prayer chain for local prayer needs, as most Baptist churches do, but Susan had been looking for a way to involve women who care about missions but who truly do not have time to attend meetings of Baptist Women.

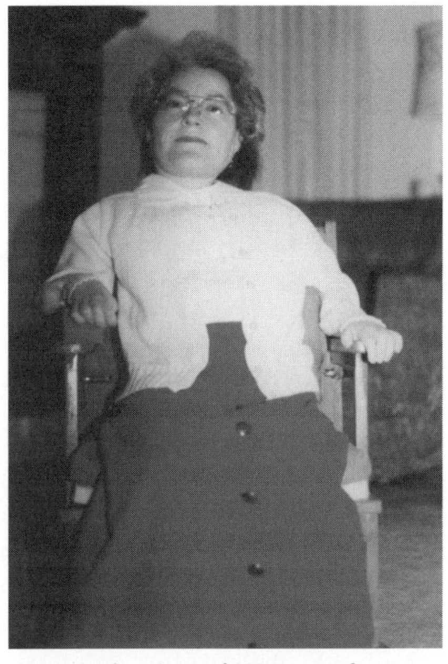

Susan in the winter of 1991 at age forty-two. She had finally become a "little grannie" to the children who invariably asked why she was confined to a respirator and chair.

Each Monday, she called the five ladies who headed the prayer groups to fill them in on current mission prayer needs. Finding prayer requests was easy through the Foreign and Home Mission Boards' toll-free prayer lines. She also culled prayer needs from the state Baptist paper, associational newsletters, and the church's own mission action ministries. By Susan coordinating all these requests and dispersing them through the five prayer group leaders, the large number of women who were taking part could use their time fully in specific prayer for specific needs. In October 1994, Susan submitted an article entitled "Reaching Out Through a Mission Prayer Chain" to *Dimension* magazine, a publication for all WMU and church mission leaders. It was accepted for future publication.

CECIL. Although she had made some definite contributions to Baptist life, Susan was reluctant to be in the spotlight herself. During her latter teen and adult years, she avoided publicity, her exceptions being expressions of her faith and the key causes central to her values in life. In 1974, Dr. Grady Cothen, then president of the Southern Baptist Sunday School

Board, came to visit Susan, asking her consent to have her story written for a book. He assured her he would allow her the privilege of approving the author chosen. When she declined, Grady asked her why. Her answer was, "I'm just not willing to live with that much publicity."

CHARLENE. Susan remained very youthful in appearance throughout her life. She was quite small, not much larger than a six or seven year old. Most of the time when children asked about her, they would say, "Mama, what happened to that little girl?" Once, however, when we were eating at a McDonald's in San Angelo, a little boy saw Susan and tugged at his grandmother's skirt. "Grandma, what happened to that little Grandma?" Susan chuckled at his remark. "Well, now! I guess I've finally grown up!" By this time, her hair had indeed begun to show a good bit of gray.

CECIL. Susan enjoyed her hobbies: painting, drawing, and cross-stitching. She did these on a little frame mounted on a movable desk which I had designed and built for her. With her right hand and arm suspended in a sling, she painted and drew the most delicate work; with her needle clutched between her fingers up against her knuckles, she embroidered. Today, several of her numbered paintings hang in our den and in my study.

CHARLENE. Perhaps a more detailed description will help. The motorized desk she used was especially designed by Cecil to fit her range of motion. It had a panel that would move from side to side and up and down. She adjusted the side-to-side movement with a head switch, and the up-and-down movement with toe and heel switches operated by her

Susan's two-inch range of motion allowed her to paint by number, a feat she accomplished beautifully, with great care. It usually took her several months to complete a painting. Nearly a dozen adorn the walls of the Ray home in Georgetown, Texas.

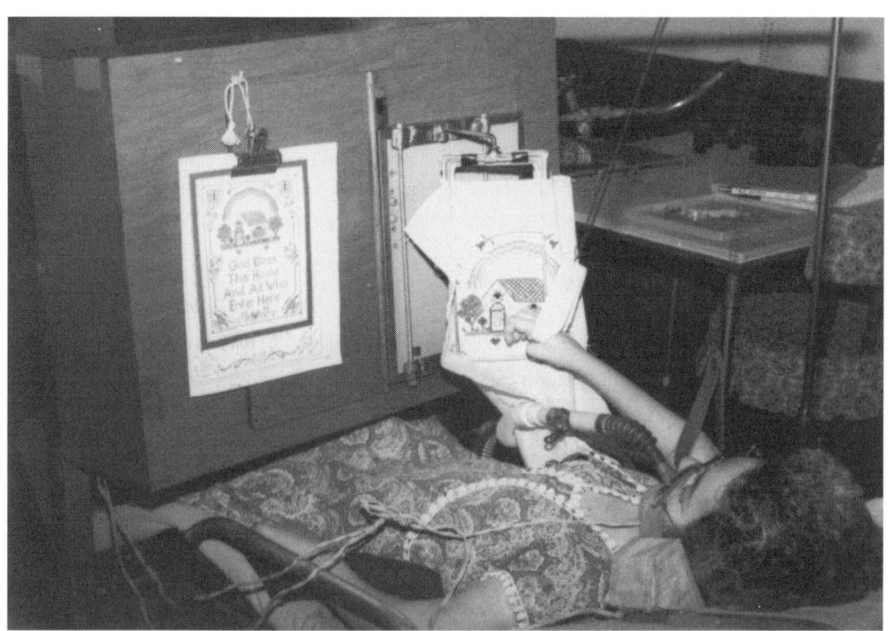

With a series of pulleys, slings, and clips, Susan cross-stitched intricate samplers and made a large number of Christmas ornaments for her church and friends.

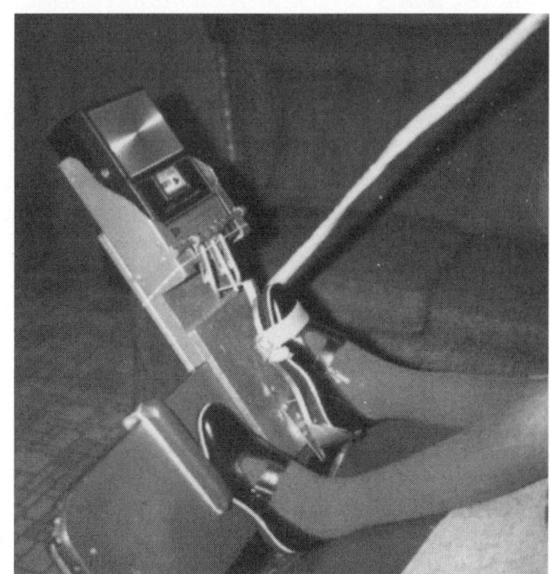

Special foot switches, custom designed to fit her capabilities, helped Susan make use of the slight movement she had.

right foot. These small movements allowed Susan to position the canvas she was painting, or the cross-stitch piece as the case might be, to the small center area where she had accurate control. She also used this movement of the panel to allow her to dip her brush in the paint and return to the focal point of control. Her needlework involved having someone thread her needle for her. Both crafts required slow and precise movements and more patience than most people have in a lifetime.

CECIL. The time and effort Susan put into her handcrafted projects made her most appreciative of the work of others. Her Aunt Lois, wife of my oldest brother, Truett, made beautiful strings of Christmas lights using turkey egg shells. A set of her "egg lights" took months of work and were both beautiful and quite valuable. She gave Susan three of them—one on a stand. Susan treasured them and would have liked very much to have a whole string, but knew it was too much for Lois to include anyone beyond her own children and grandchildren. One Christmas, a special delivery package came for Aunt Lois's "newest grandchild." Susan was elated. She refused to have them on the tree to share the spotlight with other decorations, so I strung them across the mantle where Susan never grew tired of viewing them.

Later, Susan wrote an article about her Aunt Lois and her many children and grandchildren who have followed her example in serving their churches through the years by working with babies and small children. The article was published in the Texas **Baptist Standard** *in 1994.*

CHARLENE. In mid-February 1995, Susan took a slight cold, which soon developed into pneumonia. We had been told this was among her greatest dangers and had lived in fear of it for forty-three years. Cecil and I had always agreed that we must outlive Susan because we could not bear the idea of her struggling to manage without us. Early that February morning, as we sat outside her hospital room and watched the emergency team try to save her, we were not ready at all.

Susan had been very quiet the past two days with little to say. Her heartbeat was quite fast—not erratic, just fast. For nearly two weeks, it had registered 190 beats per minute. They had finally gotten it down to 130 beats, which was still quite high. She was anxious to get out of her iron lung as early as possible each morning and told me, "Baby has always been my security, but now I just dread being put in. It's like being in a prison." She sensed she was losing ground and expressed this to her respiratory therapist, who assured her she was improving. She replied, "Michael, if I'm doing so well, then why do I feel so bad?"

Susan's firsthand knowledge of the time and talent it takes to do crafts made her most appreciative of the "turkey eggshell" Christmas lights made for her by her Aunt Lois.

The night before, the doctor had assured us that Susan was improving and would be released to go home in just a day or two. One thing, though, caused us to be concerned—Susan's ability to frog breathe had left her. She had depended on this technique to help her breathe and speak since she was a child, and she was greatly distressed at the loss. Even so, we thought she was better, but Susan disagreed.

CECIL. The trip we had made earlier to Duke Hospital had helped me reevaluate the impact of Susan's ability to frog breathe when the doctor there spent so much time listening and feeling Susan's diaphragm. He was totally fascinated; he had never seen anyone who could swallow air to that degree and use it to talk. I think it was then that I realized anew that this was God's special gift that gave Susan forty years of productive life. She could not remember back to the early days before she had developed this ability, but, for the first time, she thought she had lost it. I'm not sure she had really lost it—I think she was simply too weak to use it, but I again realized that when God bestowed that gift, it transformed her from someone with only a few months to live into a lively, vibrant person.

As close as we had become over the years, Charlene and I could usually sense when things weren't just right, but, to be honest, this time I didn't think Susan was as critical as she was. The pneumonia was clearing up, and I thought the frog breathing would come back as she gained strength. Susan didn't.

CHARLENE. "I think I'm dying, Mama," Susan had told me that night as I was preparing her for bed.

"Oh, no," I said. "The doctor says you're doing better. We'll be home before you know it." Later, as I lay down to sleep, I prayed, "Not now, Lord. Not now!"

About five o'clock the next morning, I was awakened by the emergency crew pulling her iron lung out into the hall and starting resuscitation efforts, but to no avail. Those watching her heart monitor said there was one perfect beat—then nothing.

The Lord had answered, "Yes, now!"

Susan was placed in an iron lung on February 27, 1952. We laid her to rest on February 27, 1995. For forty-three years she had been our treasure. Her needs had defined our lives, her accomplishments had given added purpose to our own calling. And oh, what memories she has left us!

CECIL. Susan was never able to travel beyond the boundaries of her own country, but she carried the whole world in her heart. Her quest for knowledge, her intense study of world events, her interest in the people of various nations, and her concern for their spiritual welfare all transported her to places she never got to visit in person. Polio had set the physical limits of her existence, but her indomitable spirit and her faith defied these limits to include the whole world.

CHARLENE. The last writing assignment Susan had was to help update a textbook on Baptist polity for students in our Texas Baptist colleges and universities. She completed and mailed the first assignment just before going to the hospital. We have received word from the publishers that the book, *Baptist History, Distinctives and Work Relations*, has been dedicated to Susan's memory.

13
Dancing for the King

Susan had no idea how remarkable her accomplishments were and would have been embarrassed to have anyone tell her so. She radiated a feeling of confidence in herself and of sincere interest in everyone she met, apparently seeing little difference between herself and them. Her first and most difficult embroidered panel sets forth what may have been her philosophy:

> God Grant Me the Serenity to
> Accept the Things I Cannot Change,
> the Courage to Change the Things I Can,
> And the Wisdom to Know the Difference.

Today, a wallhanging which captures her spirit and attitude still graces her home. It reads:

> God Bless this House and
> All who Enter Here

Her cross-stitched Christmas decorations adorn trees at Crabtree Valley Baptist Church in Raleigh and Crestview Baptist Church in Georgetown each year. Many of her friends treasure ornaments made and shared by Susan and assign them a special place during the Christmas holidays. Her original drawing and cross-stitch of "The Little Engine That Could" hangs in the office of Dr. Thorkild Engen, director of the Orthotics Department of the Texas Institute for Rehabilitation and Research in Houston. It proudly proclaims:

> "I Thought I Could!"

and she did!

CECIL. One of Susan's crusades related to the need for wholesome television programming. When any of the networks produced and aired a good show or series, they got a letter from Susan thanking them, or sometimes scolding them, for programs she considered unworthy. In the weeks following Susan's death, we were all startled to hear the announcer of a local station say, ". . . perhaps Susan Ray of Georgetown says it best. . . ." Then Susan's note appeared on screen, commending them for rerunning wholesome family programs such as *I Love Lucy*, *Gomer Pyle*, and others. At the end of her note, the station cut to a scene of Gomer saying his famous "thank you, thank you, thank you." Weeks later, this promo was still being shown—and thus a small bit of Susan's ministry lives on.

CHARLENE. Susan's only unfinished writing project was a freelance exploration of the history and widespread use of the little "Apple Tract." This little tract tells about the man to whom God gave ten apples, but the man gave back to God only the core. Used extensively on the mission field to illustrate stewardship principles, those apples became bananas, mangos, corn, or whatever made the tract relevant to local ministry. After her death, a letter came from the historian of the American Baptist Convention telling of their use of the tract at one of their conventions. I had to write a note of thanks, but regret, that the "History of the Apple" tract will not be finished . . . or will it? Maybe someone one else. . . .

When Susan's death became known, messages of condolence and hope were sent to the Rays from all over the country. On March 5, 1995, an article by Beth Pratt in the **Lubbock Avalanche-Journal** *expressed the way those who had known her through the years felt about Susan:*

> Courage is a quality that we relate to heroic actions rather than to the routine of our daily lives. But some of the greatest acts of courage are by people such as Susan and her parents.

Orville Scott of the Baptist General Convention of Texas said:

> [Susan] will be remembered for her determination and courage and for her life of service.

Joshua Grijalva, former dean and president of Susan's beloved Hispanic Baptist Theological Seminary, wrote:

. . . And what a giant she grew to be in the Lord. Her painful body is at rest, but her joy, works and inspiration—these will remain until eternity. You were both good missionary trainers, and in Susan, you developed the highest and utmost to His glory.

In expressing his sorrow at Susan's passing, Cecil Sherman of the Cooperative Baptist Fellowship wrote:

In all of my life, I have never seen anybody will to be useful, to make a difference, like Susan. She was not given as much as the rest of us. Her body did not serve her as ours do. But she was not put down! She made a difference!

Roy Smith, head of the Baptist State Convention of North Carolina, who assisted in Susan's funeral, pretty much summed it up:

The word "handicapped" was not in Susan's vocabulary. She faced all of life with courage and faith in God. She was a "missionary extraordinaire."

And knowing of her concern for governmental affairs, Smith also said:

Susan Ray wrote to more policy makers than any other person I know. She accepted, personally, and at face value, the words of Jesus when He said, "As the Father hath sent me, even so I have sent you into the world."

The Executive Boards of the Baptist General Convention of Texas and the Baptist State Convention of North Carolina both passed tributes to the life of this one small person as well.

CECIL. In July, six months after Susan's death, we received a Texas Senate Proclamation in memory of Susan. Susan had been corresponding with Senator Jim Turner concerning a number of bills, one of which was the concealed weapons bill. He knew Susan was adamantly opposed, and his letters reflected his appreciation for her concern and explained why he supported the bill. I answered his last letter, explaining that Susan had died and thanked him for his courtesy. I would not have been surprised at a personal letter from him, but was very surprised with the Resolution of Appreciation from the Texas Senate. This was a fitting tribute to Susan, coming as it did from someone she had both supported and challenged on a number of occasions. Senator Turner wrote:

It is with a great deal of sadness that I extend to you Senate Proclamation Number 208, honoring the memory of your daughter, Susan. Please accept it as a token of my deepest sympathy.

Susan will long be remembered by all who knew her as a dedicated and caring individual. Her life leaves behind many wonderful memories for her friends and family to share. The Senate of the State of Texas joins your family in mourning this great loss

SENATE PROCLAMATION
in Memory
of
Susan Ray

WHEREAS, The Senate of the State of Texas was saddened to learn of the death of Susan Ray of Georgetown, who died February 25, 1995, at the age of 47; and

WHEREAS, Susan was the daughter of Dr. and Mrs. Cecil Ray of Georgetown; and

WHEREAS, She will be remembered for her life of service and for her courage and determination; and

WHEREAS, Stricken by polio at age four, Susan was a quadriplegic and was dependent on an iron lung; during the first years of her illness, her father invented many of the machines that made a meaningful and productive life possible for his daughter; and

WHEREAS, Susan dedicated herself to missionary work while attending a summer program at Glorieta Baptist Assembly; and

WHEREAS, This courageous and determined young woman was the author of the book, *The Baptist Way*, and the co-author of three books, *Baptists Working Together, Cooperation, the Baptist Way* and *The Witnessing, Giving Life*; and,

WHEREAS, She wrote numerous articles for newspapers and magazines and scripts for filmstrips and a movie; she was particularly interested in issues concerning the worth and dignity of the individual, the environment and conservation; and

102

WHEREAS, Susan established a permanent place for herself in the hearts of those she loved, and the example of courage and tenacity with which she lived her life will be her lasting legacy to her loved ones; now, therefore be it

PROCLAIMED, That the Senate of the State of Texas hereby extend sincere condolences to her family: her parents, Dr. and Mrs. Cecil Ray; her brother, Dr. Lanny Ray; and a niece and nephew, Jennifer Ray and Michael Ray; and be it further

PROCLAIMED, That a copy of this Proclamation be prepared for her family as an expression of sympathy from the Texas Senate.

The influence of Susan's life is continuing. In April 1996, eleven years after the Rays moved from North Carolina back to Texas, Crabtree Valley Baptist Church celebrated their twenty-fifth anniversary. In that program, entitled "Precious Memories," Bill Baxley told how Susan Ray had been chosen as the best person to embody the spirit of the occasion. Listing the places she served and remembering the influence Susan had on his family as well as the entire church, Baxley said:

Memories of Susan are still meaningful to us today. She was one tiny lady with one giant spirit! Although unable to walk, she believed there was no mountain she could not climb. On behalf of all past and present members and all who will come in the future, we dedicate and pay tribute to Susan Ray.

CHARLENE. Although her range of motion was limited, Susan's life experiences were many and varied. She could say, "I've been to the top of Pike's Peak and to the bottom of Carlsbad Caverns. I've been from San Francisco to Miami Beach. We saw Ruby Falls in Tennessee and the Seven Falls and Garden of the Gods in Colorado. We even rode a small train into an old gold mine. I saw Old Faithful from my tiny tank because I had a cold, but I saw it!

"When we lived in North Carolina, I went up Grandfather Mountain and down to Nag's Head where the Wright brothers learned to fly. I saw the Cape Hatteras Lighthouse which stands guard on the Outer Banks, the graveyard of the Atlantic. I rode the Blue Ridge Parkway and toured Williamsburg in Virginia. We even visited Epcot Center in Florida and made many, many trips back to Texas while living in Raleigh."

Susan's life was varied and filled with meaning because her parents planned that she would experience a full, rich life in spite of her handicaps.

However, to a large degree, Susan's life was determined by Susan herself. She stated her own views about life when she said:

When I think of Helen Keller, I think of a great woman who overcame great handicaps. I join others in admiring her for this, but when I think of President Franklin Roosevelt, I think first of a great president of the United States and only second as a person with handicaps. I would far rather be remembered for what I can contribute than for having handicaps.

That Susan succeeded in her wish is evidenced by a number of those who knew her. A May 1966 article in the missions magazine, **The Window,** *by writer Judy Hawkins of Forest Park, Georgia, expresses this quite well:*

I thought about how much Susan's life has influenced my life and that of others. She has so much inner strength to spare that it seems to overflow into other people's lives.

In the April 1986 issue of **Royal Service,** *Frances Riley shared an interview with Susan that reflects the same strengths:*

Call her a remarkable woman, and Susan Ray's eyes will flash with indignation, but only for a moment. She will be too busy learning about you and your interests to give your description more than a passing thought.

Susan says she never lets her limitations decide what projects she will attempt—only the methods she uses to accomplish them.

CECIL. Susan still had much to do. Her last cross-stitch is unfinished; it is an American flag. Her role in getting out information on prayer needs, through the missionary prayer chain she designed, is not finished. Her support for all her good causes is not finished. There was so much more for Susan to do, but we know she is with God. At Susan's funeral, her former pastor, Stuart DePew, expressed something of how we feel:

Her doll-like feet in unscuffed shoes are scuffed today. The frail body that could not breathe in earth's air is now breathing the fragrance of eternity. The secret of Susan's strength and power must have been that she had a clear knowledge of the reward that would be hers.

CHARLENE. Since Christmas of 1994, two months before Susan's death, we had been expecting a call from our dear African friend, Douglas Waruta, to tell us he had arrived back in the States. He was coming to Hardin-Simmons as a visiting professor for a series of lectures. On Saturday, February 25, Douglas called to tell us he had arrived at Fort Worth and would go to the university on Monday. I told him that Susan had died that morning.

Missionary friends brought Douglas over to be with our family, for we had all remained close through the years, and it was a great comfort to us that Douglas was able to take part in Susan's funeral service. That would have meant a great deal to Susan as well. Susan and Douglas were dear and close friends, sharing a deeper understanding than most people experience. He expressed that love in these remarks he made at her funeral:

> When I came to America, I found many wonderful surprises, but the most precious and sweetest was to see a lovely human being in a tank! I did not believe a human being could live like that!

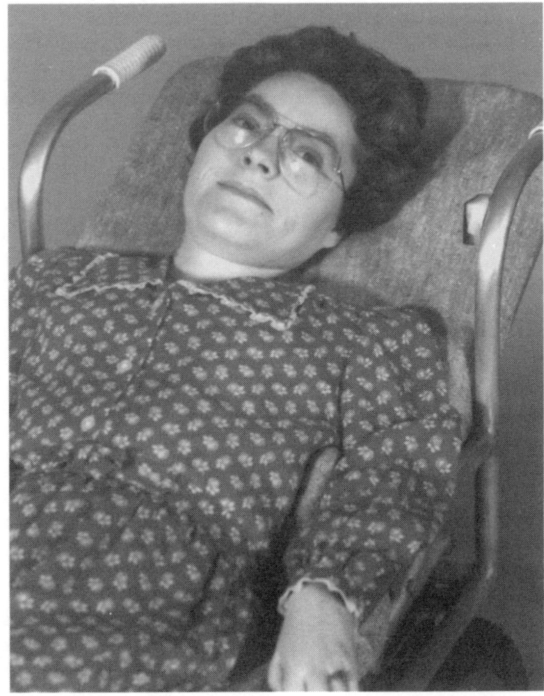

Susan's last portrait. As always, her smile predominates all else.

I looked at Susan—I bent to greet her and saw her face full of calmness —and joy—and serenity—and peace. From that very moment, Susan and I became the greatest of friends. We talked and joked and fellow-shipped together in some of the best moments of my life.

America is a land of many surprises, but the surprise of a life like Susan's will never be forgotten. I want you to know that the work she has done has reached all over the world.

All I can tell you today is summed up in one word—continue! Continue to care, continue to love, continue to pray! Embrace God's light that was in Susan all these years. The greatest tribute we can give to Susan is to continue those very things she lived for. We must continue, because what she lived for will never die!

If Susan were here, she would still be involved in seeking solutions to life's problems. The ozone layer, world hunger, the erosion of trust in our nation's leaders. All these and more would be on her agenda.

She would be aware that polio has still not been eradicated from our world; indeed is becoming more prevalent in undeveloped nations. She would have read about little David Salamone who had barely learned to crawl when he got polio—from the very vaccination that was supposed to protect him. It's a nightmare that happens to about eight Americans each year who are given the oral polio vaccine which is composed of weakened but live virus. Yet this is the only vaccine that produces immunity in the intestine, where the polio virus grows before it causes paralysis.

Susan would know that a new program of immunization will become effective in January 1997 which changes the current four doses of live oral vaccine to two shots of inactive vaccine and two doses of live oral treatment. Hopefully, this will keep youngsters like David Salamone from contracting the disease—ever!

Just as Susan would be concerned for the spiritual poverty and little knowledge of Christ that reigns in much of the world, she would also know that polio has still not been eradicated. It is present in a number of Asian and African countries. Former President Jimmy Carter, who returned from Nyamme, Sudan, in 1995, named guinea worms and polio as the major health problems there. Both are caused by the polluted river which is the only source of drinking water available. Susan the world citizen would know that the danger of a worldwide epidemic of the disease that changed her life forever is still eminent, and Susan the missionary would be crusading for someone to change things for the better.

CHARLENE. Susan's iron lungs have been donated to "Friend Ships," a Christian nonprofit corporation, manned totally by volunteers, which operates a fleet of sea-going vessels supplying life-support systems, nutritious foods, and other humanitarian goods to areas of need all over the world.

Susan's typewriter has gone to a rheumatic woman who was formally a legal secretary. Her humidifier went to a Catholic priest, who is also a polio victim. Her gasoline generator, which provided backup during power failures, has been given away.

Susan's paintings still grace the walls of our home, her cross-stitch pieces still echo her philosophy of life and her determination to make a difference, but the remarkable person who was our beloved daughter is no longer there.

She is free!

The King's Daughter Dances

Mama, I'm home!
The wings of an angel bore me here
    and laid me down at the foot of my Father's throne.

He smiled at me and said,
"My daughter, stand up!"
And I stood before Him in awe and wonder!

He said, "Welcome home, my child."
Then He opened wide His arms and I ran,
Mama, I *ran* into His embrace!

There were tears, like tiny pearls, in His eyes
But they were tears of love and joy
Because now, Mama, I am healed!

My Father said, "Dance for me, my child," and I answered,
"Father, I have never learned to dance."
Did you know, Mama, that God can laugh?
It was like rolling thunder and a rainbow, joined together
    in a glorious celebration, just for me.

He said, "Daughter, here you do not need to learn.
If I bid you dance to My glory, your feet will know," and so I danced.
I twirled on my toes! I floated like a cloud! I leapt like a mountain goat!

All the while, the angels played their golden harps and sang
    and the saints swayed to the rhythm and clapped their hands.
Oh, Mama, I wish you could have seen me!

So many times I wondered "why?"
You said, "One day, you'll understand 'why' but now, Mama, I'll tell
   you a secret,
Here, in the midst of rapture and laughter and singing, the 'why' no
   longer matters."

I have all eternity to run—and skip—and dance in my Father's
   house, my home!

Betty D. Mojica
February 25, 1995

Appendix: Equipment List of Susan's "Enablers"

Tank respirators (called iron lungs), positive pressure ventilators, chest shell negative pressure respirators, rocking beds, special reclining chairs, motorized desks for painting, drawing, cross-stitching, special telephone dialing adaptations, tape recorder operations, specially equipped cars and vans with wheelchair loading helps—all were major components of equipment Susan used to make her life full and productive.

Although these many pieces of equipment played a large part in her life, they are only a small part of Susan's story. She saw her equipment as tools for breaking down barriers, enabling her to pursue her goals and be fully involved with life.

Susan's story is more about determination and a strong desire to be involved with life and to make a difference. The significance of each piece of equipment was not its attractiveness, or lack thereof, but rather its contribution to Susan in her quest for living.

TANK RESPIRATOR UNITS

Each tank respirator unit was built to serve a special purpose. The function of the tank respirator, often called an iron lung, is to help replace normal diaphragm functions for the intake and exhalation of air. The person lies in the tank with the head outside on a head rest. A rubber collar and soft neck wrap keep air from escaping. The breathing rate is determined by the needs and age of the individual, usually somewhere between eleven and twenty-eight breaths per minute. Air is drawn into the lungs as the tank's bellows create a vacuum inside the tank. This action permits the individual to experience a near-normal intake of air. This pulling in of air is referred to as "negative pressure."

1. Susan's "Baby Tank," so named by Susan, was built in Lubbock in the spring of 1953 about eight months after she returned home to Lubbock from the hospital in Houston. It was built before small travel tanks were available commercially. This first travel tank was built to meet a travel crisis involving Susan's six-hundred-mile return to the Houston hospital for a check-up.

Baby Tank was built of steel and equipped with two motors—one a twelve-volt dc unit to operate the unit during travel and the other a 120 ac unit for home use. It opened from the side like a trunk, weighed about 120 pounds, and originally had removable legs to fit into our car or van.

Following our return home, Baby became Susan's at-home, everyday use tank. The large Emerson tank provided by the March of Dimes was kept for a few months as a backup, but once the home-built unit proved durable, the Emerson tank was returned to the March of Dimes. Baby Tank served her for forty-three years, up to and including the night she died in the Georgetown hospital.

2. The Alligator Tank was so named by Susan because it hinged at the back and opened "wide like the mouth of an alligator." Built in 1955, it was used for almost ten years for overnight travel involving motels or at grandparents' homes. It was operated by a separate respirator pump unit connected to the tank by an air hose, either the commercially made Huxley or a similar homemade unit.

3. The Miniature Tank was smaller than Susan's other units. It was placed on her chairbed and was operated by a hose connected to a pump unit. This unit was used for special needs and special trips, such as the time the family vacationed at Yellowstone Park. Susan took a severe cold on that trip, which always posed a danger to her, but was still able to sightsee by riding in this small tank with it resting on her chair.

Constructed of fiberglass, this tank only weighed twenty-five pounds, which enabled Cecil to carry it with Susan already in it. A unique feature was the collar design which fastened to the top and was laid over Susan and then fitted around her neck to create a seal. "You don't get into this one," Susan said, "you put it on!"

4. Plywood Tank was built in the late 1960s while the family lived in Grand Prairie, Texas. Another family had borrowed Susan's small travel trailer and the Alligator Tank when the family decided to visit both sets of grandparents in San Angelo for a few days. This small tank, with folding legs, was built during afterwork hours in just one week. It rode on a carriage rack on the trunk lid.

While intended as a temporary unit for this one weekend use, it turned out to be very efficient. Susan enjoyed this small tank so much that it was used again for a few times and then given to the family that had borrowed the other tank. It also became the working model for another wooden tank to be built later on.

5. Fiberglass Tank was built in 1965 with fold-up legs to allow it to fit into a special compartment in Susan's newly built aluminum equipment trailer. This tank was operated by either the Huxley or the similar home-made unit, so both units were carried on trips in order to have a standby. This backup plan proved to be valuable on several occasions, and this unit continued to be a part of Susan's special equipment for the rest of her life.

6. Wooden Tank was designed to fit into the twenty-two-foot Shasta travel trailer, which was redesigned inside to accommodate Susan's tank and travel chair, and to firmly anchor the travel tank while en route. During her last fifteen years, Susan used this wooden tank and travel trailer on many family trips. She liked this tank well enough that she chose to use it during her two-week stay at Rex Hospital in Raleigh.

7. The Tank That Failed. While in Lubbock, Cecil built one tank that never worked. It would have been Tank #2, but instead it went to the junk pile. More time and money went into this "monstrosity" than any two of the other units. While it was a failure and was discarded, it taught a good lesson in things that would not work.

CHEST SHELL RESPIRATORS

The chest shell, like the iron lung, is a negative pressure unit. Susan used the chest shell for daytime respiratory help during the ten-year period from 1952 to 1962. She wore the chest shell under her blouse, with a hose connecting the shell to the pump unit.

At first, she was able to be out of the iron lung for only a few hours each day; however, this was gradually increased so that she used the iron lung for sleeping only. During the day, she used the chest shell part of the time and the rocking chair part of the time, following a time schedule for the use of each.

Since both the chest shell and the iron lung were negative pressure units, Susan was using the pull of negative pressure both day and night. Her doctors in Houston became concerned that this was causing her chest to enlarge too much, which might eventually create greater breathing problems. In 1962, when the new positive pressure units were introduced, Susan was given a new unit—one that changed her daytime breathing pattern from negative to positive pressure.

Had Susan lived, her next planned step was to move completely away from the use of her iron lung to the use of a nose mask, operated by a positive pressure unit. She felt it was urgent to end the use of the iron lung because of increasing complications from the long use of negative pull. She even tried using the new positive pressure system briefly while in the Georgetown hospital, but was already too ill to consider the change at that time.

POSITIVE PRESSURE RESPIRATORS
(Also Called Ventilators)

Positive pressure respirators, increasingly referred to as ventilators, provide respiratory aid by blowing in air through a hose and mouthpiece. From 1962 to 1993, Susan used a positive pressure unit, first made by Thompson and generally referred to as a Bantam. By the late 1980s, these units were rapidly becoming obsolete and were being replaced with new, very complex positive pressure ventilators. Realizing that the Bantam units were being phased out, a search began to acquire workable parts for replacement positive pressure units.

Cecil had already started experimenting with this when the Rays received notice that the rental price would double the next month. This provided the encouragement needed to perfect a unit that he could build and maintain. Cecil built a test model designed for twelve-volt dc operation to be used in the travel van. This test model worked smoothly and established the fact that Susan responded well to such a piston-driven positive pressure unit.

Prior to this time, the inability to find electric motors that were satisfactory in performance had been a major obstacle to Cecil's building such a unit. Now, however, several new electric motors, both ac and dc, became available, making the transition to homemade units workable. Cecil built an ac operated unit with a sigh-breath attachment which automatically produced three deep breaths every thirty seconds. This was followed by a backup unit. The next step was to build a dc unit which fortunately came at the time that some new dc motor and speed control units were introduced. This dc unit worked very well in the car during travel but, more significantly, proved to have a remarkable capacity for use on a small dc battery—like the ones used in a riding lawn mower.

With this small battery, Susan could use this unit up to thirty-three hours on one battery charge. This was in contrast to the three–four hours supplied by the Bantam, which also required the use of a large car battery. The only maintenance required for these units was a simple checkup every five–six weeks and a few drops of oil on the moving parts. Susan used these units for about eighteen months prior to her death.

Because of the efficiency and trouble-free characteristics of these new units, Cecil soon realized he had built more than were needed.

CHAIRS AND ATTACHMENTS

Chairs for Susan provided two very basic helps. Comfort and proper posture were the first priorities; next was providing functional assistance to Susan in her multiple daily activities. These enablers provided help in getting her dressed for the day, and in the pursuit of her many interests, which included telephoning, reading, writing, typing, painting, cross-stitching, and drawing. Chairs with numerous attachments were designed to enable her to do each of these tasks.

Like her various breathing units, Susan's chairs were developed as needs arose, and were discarded when obsolete, worn out, or outgrown. These multipurpose chairs were as important to Susan's ability to do things as her breathing units were to sustain her life.

Susan's everyday chair underwent many changes. First built as a chair-size rocking bed, it had features much like those of modern hospital beds. In time this chair, that started as a combination reclining and rocking chair, was changed to a reclining chair with elevator action that allowed its height to be altered for help in dressing each morning and then adjusted for whatever activities we chose to do.

This chair with many lives was never considered finished since both slight and major changes were frequently made and new attachments added to meet Susan's ever-expanding interests and activities. In the 1980s, when her doctor determined she could sit at a 45-degree angle, this chair was again slightly altered to accommodate the change, making it easier for her to watch television and participate in other activities.

Equally important to Susan was her lightweight aluminum "away-from-home" chair. This chair was used for church, shopping, vacation trips, eating out, and tours of the yard, so Susan could keep tabs on the flowers and plants she loved so well. Space under the chair was used for her positive pressure units. With the development of the homebuilt positive pressure units and the twelve-volt dc units, Susan was able to use this chair powered with a small battery. Not having to depend on the availability of a plug-in made attending church and other outings much easier.

In the long process of coming to these two chairs with their multiple functions, Susan had used and phased out numerous other chairs that had assisted her to this point. These earlier chair versions included:

1. A small-size copy of a reclining lawn chair. Five-year-old Susan was almost lost in adult-size chairs, so Cecil built a smaller version to fit her.

2. An experimental outdoor chair with two wheels in back and one in front. It was not stable and was the one Lanny accidentally turned over, giving Susan her black eye.

3. A multipurpose chair, built in 1958 of lightweight tubing, was Cecil's first attempt at welding aluminum. It had two wheel bases: one for outdoor use with large wheels like those on wheelchairs, and later, another smaller wheel base for use as a travel chair. When used with the large wheel base, this chair could also function as a "rocking bed" and as Susan's "going-to-church" chair in San Antonio. After learning that the wide wheel base would not allow them to get through doors in some stores and restaurants, Cecil fashioned the smaller base on caster-type wheels. This chair weighed about sixty pounds.

4. A motor chair, built in 1959 as Susan's Christmas "bike," was designed for independent "whizzing" all over inside the house and on sidewalks. This chair was built of aluminum tubing and powered by a twelve-volt battery and motors which were operated by special switches Cecil designed to fit Susan's slight range of motion. A foot pedal worked reversible motors for forward and backward drive by means of her heel or toe. Extremely sensitive microswitches ran the motors for right and left turns, accomplished by a slight forward or backward motion of her right hand.

5. A bath chair of plastic tubing, with tent-awning tape for lattice, was built for use in the tub or on a frame at tub edge level.

DESKS

1. Although Susan's arm movements, when using the arm-bar and sling, allowed an in-out swing of about ten inches, she could only work in a small area of not more than a two-inch square. This movable desk surface made it possible for Susan to write over almost the entire area of a sheet of paper. She used this desk for drawing, cross-stitching, painting, and writing. It was constructed of a steel-tubing frame on wheels with a wooden desk surface on a metal frame with a movable panel-on-panel for

two-way movement. Microswitches on either side of Susan's head moved the small panel up and down. Microswitches under the heel and toe of her right foot moved the large panel right and left.

2. A clip-on desk, built in 1953 and rebuilt in 1960, fastened onto the arms of Susan's reclining chair. She used it for reading, looking at pictures, and playing games. This desk clipped onto the chair arms with trunk catches.

ASPIRATORS

1. An ac aspirator was built in 1959 from a small paint sprayer with a vacuum hose attached and bottle added.

2. A dc aspirator was made from a car electric windshield wiper unit. It was used only while in the car.

CAR LOADING AID

The ability to sideload Susan and her chair was made possible by having the back door rehinged at its back, with the dividing post cut away and permanently attached to the back door. An interior platform on the passenger's side was seven feet long, adequate to accommodate any of her iron lungs or chairs.

Beginning in 1987, Susan had a commercially built Golden Boy swing lift that allowed her and her wheelchair to be lifted from ground level and swung inside where her chair was anchored to the floor. In 1992, Susan also had a homemade swing lift for use with the family's Dodge Caravan. Because of the limited space, this lift platform was made smaller—just allowing the exact width of her travel chair.

VEHICLES FOR TRAVEL

Travel to areas local and beyond required customized vehicles that were uniquely equipped for Susan's comfort and respiratory assistance. Trips involving overnight stay also required iron lung equipment for sleeping, plus special chairs.

Adapted vehicles over the years included station wagons, used limousines, two-door sedans, and a van. A used Dodge limousine and two Ford station wagons were modified with the passenger side back door rehinged to the rear side of the door and the dividing post removed and attached to the back of the door. This allowed an opening of about six feet which permitted the loading of Susan in her chair or, as needed, Susan in her travel lung.

From 1953 to 1965, these special features were essential as Susan frequently traveled in her iron lung tank. The last emergency trip requiring the use of an iron lung came in 1958 when Susan was rushed from San Antonio to Houston for emergency surgery.

From 1965 to 1987, Susan's transportation involved using two-door cars with the passenger front seat removed and a platform built to cover the space from the back seat to the dashboard. Her travel chairs could be fitted into this space and anchored in place by front and back hooks to the floor. Susan's chair was fitted with a seat belt, so she had double protection of being anchored to her chair and her chair being anchored to the floor.

From 1987 on, Susan's main transportation involved the use of a full-size van that had been customized to provide safety anchors for her chair, a Golden Boy wheelchair lift, and an electrical plug-in for her twelve-volt dc respirator. In 1990, the family's dodge Caravan was modified with a built-in platform and similar chairlift to provide an alternate travel vehicle.

TYPEWRITERS

1. Typewriters were central to Susan's special mission in life. An IBM typewriter repairman in San Antonio worked with Cecil to design and build her first unit. Instead of having keys, her keyboard was a series of holes into which she would push a stylus to activate a solenoid, which would then push the selected key on the typewriter. All the keyholes had to fit into a space no more than one and one-half inches high and three and three-quarters inches wide. The keyboard was arranged so the most frequently used keys were easiest to reach.

2. Susan's second typewriter was an adaptation of an IBM Selectric which enabled her to choose various fonts and sizes. Cecil designed this version without assistance, building a box of solenoids which sat on top of the keyboard with each one acting like a finger when Susan pushed her stylus into the hole allotted to that letter. It worked perfectly about eighty percent of the time, but often behaved as if some small demon were playing tricks on Susan. When Lanny came home one weekend from graduate school in Austin, he saw the problem and in less than thirty

minutes had searched through his "hobby boxes," replaced a wire in the electric stabilizer, and corrected the problem. Susan used this typewriter for over eight years.

3. Her third typewriter was an electronic Olivette. The keyboard wiring was designed and installed by Glen Starling, a member of the Baptist State Convention staff in Raleigh. Just as the emerging electronics area opened countless opportunities for almost everyone, it brought better typing options for Susan. This unit proved to be similar to her others, but the electronics were more effective. Susan had only to touch a key to make contact rather than activating a solenoid which activated a key.

This typewriter also had a Spanish keyboard which she used to write articles for the *El Bautista Mexicano* and for the Christmas drama which won second place in a Spanish Publishing House contest that involved participants from North and South America. Susan used this typewriter, along with a word processor, for the remaining years of her life.

4. A Smith Corona word processor was Susan's last typewriter, a unit she shared with her father. Cecil used the standard keyboard that came with the unit, and Susan again had her own remote keyboard. Lanny provided the electronics for the remote keyboard that linked Susan to the word processor. Susan's keyboard was similar in appearance to the unit built for the Olivette but was designed for the Smith Corona. The cord from Susan's keyboard was equipped with the same plug-in features as the one that came with the unit's keyboard. This permitted a closer partnership in writing projects between father and daughter since Susan continued to proofread and edit for Cecil. This allowed Susan to make corrections on the unit rather than completely retype.